Warnings FROM *Heaven*

Warnings FROM *Heaven*

VISIONS OF HEAVEN, HELL, AND THE COMING INVASION OF AMERICA

Louis Nicolosi *with* **Arthur Kerr**

WestBow
P R E S S
A DIVISION OF THOMAS NELSON

WestBow Press books may be ordered through
booksellers or by contacting:

WestBow Press
A Division of Thomas Nelson
1663 Liberty Drive
Bloomington, IN 47403
www.westbowpress.com
1-(866) 928-1240

All scripture references are taken from the
King James Version of the Bible.

ISBN: 978-1-4497-9988-5 (e)
ISBN: 978-1-4497-9989-2 (sc)

Library of Congress Control Number: 2013911886

Printed in the United States of America.

WestBow Press rev. date: 12/31/2013

Dedication

To Jesus Christ and to the praise of His glory, I devote every page of this write. The testimony of the Lord is sure, making wise the simple (Psalm 19:7). It is God who sees the future. It is He who knows the end from the beginning. It is He who divulges His secrets and mystery of things to come to His servants. O Lord my God, be glorified.

Table of Contents

Acknowledgments

In the Garden of Eden God made the man Adam. After all was made and God saw that all the works of His hands were good, He acknowledged that something was still missing. That something was someone; Eve, and she was given to Adam as his wife. It was not good for man to be alone so God made woman and gave her as help to man. I thank God for my wife Lucy. She is my life partner, and she has been by my side throughout the greater part of my journey here on earth. We have travelled and still travel many roads together, and dear Lucy is often the inspiration and pilot on our voyages. Thank you dear for just being there.

Introduction

Visions are avenues through which we are given encounters into the spirit realm. God communicates His messages and instructions to us through the channels of visions. God speaks to us in many different ways. Among other gifts, in 1 Corinthians 12:7–10 the Scripture speaks of the gift of discerning of spirits. This happens when a person's spiritual eyes are opened and he sees into the spirit realm. This person would be able to see good or bad. He could see Jesus, angels, or demons. His encounter is defined as discerning of spirits. *"But the manifestation of the Spirit is given to every man to profit withal. For to one is given by the Spirit the word of wisdom; to another the word of knowledge by the same Spirit; to another faith by the same Spirit; to another the gifts of healing by the same Spirit; to another the working of miracles; to another prophecy; to another discerning of spirits; to another divers kinds of tongues; to another the interpretation of tongues."* To my knowledge, there are three types of visions. There are dream visions, trance visions, and open visions. Let's talk about *dream* visions first.

Many people have dreams in the night season. This is where we fall asleep and are brought to consciousness by seeing into another world. We dream mainly at night not because we want to dream but because they just happen. All dream visions are not from the Lord. Some are from the demonic world. Nightmare is not from the Lord but from demons that try to open doors for the spirits of fear and demonic activities to enter into our lives. Some people rarely have any dreams while some people are always dreaming. Sometimes God Himself will give someone a revelatory message or a very important instruction in a dream vision.

In the book of Genesis, God appeared in a dream to King Abimelech to let him know and understand that Sarah, the woman he took from Abraham because he thought she was Abraham's sister, is actually Abraham's wife

(Genesis 20:2–3). *"And Abraham said of Sarah his wife, she is my sister: and Abimelech king of Gerar sent, and took Sarah. But God came to Abimelech in a dream by night, and said to him, behold, thou art but a dead man, for the woman which thou hast taken; for she is a man's wife."*

Joseph, the eleventh son of Jacob, was a dreamer. God gave him dreams concerning the future of his family's welfare and his eventual governance. *"And Joseph dreamed a dream, and he told it his brethren: and they hated him yet the more. And he said unto them, Hear, I pray you, this dream which I have dreamed: for, behold, we were binding sheaves in the field, and, lo, my sheaf arose, and also stood upright; and, behold, your sheaves stood round about, and made obeisance to my sheaf"* (Genesis 37:5–7). Here we understand that Joseph was asleep when he saw this vision.

The second vision we will look at is *trance* vision. In his experience, we see that Peter was not asleep. He went into a short spell or trance vision while praying, and he saw and heard things from heaven. When the vision was over he was back to himself. God ordained Apostle Peter to be the first Apostle to take the message of the baptism with the Holy Spirit to the Gentile nations. While Peter was in the city of Joppa he was on a house top praying. Suddenly he fell into a trance and had a vision. The Holy Spirit was directing Peter in this trance vision to take the message of the baptism with the Holy Spirit to Cornelius' household.

Cornelius was a faithful believer in God, but he was not taught nor had any experience of the baptism with the Holy Ghost (Acts 11:5–16). "*I was in the city of Joppa praying: and in a trance I saw a vision, A certain vessel descend, as it had been a great sheet, let down from heaven by four corners; and it came even to me: upon the which when I had fastened mine eyes, I considered, and saw four-footed beasts of the earth, and wild beasts, and creeping things, and fowls of the air. And I heard a voice saying unto me, Arise, Peter; slay and eat. But I said, not so, Lord: for nothing common or unclean hath at any time entered into my mouth. But the voice answered me again from heaven, what God hath cleansed, that call not thou common. And this was done three times: and all were drawn up again into heaven. And, behold, immediately there were three men already come unto the house where I was, sent from*

Caesarea unto me. And the Spirit bade me go with them, nothing doubting. Moreover these six brethren accompanied me, and we entered into the man's house: And he shewed us how he had seen an angel in his house, which stood and said unto him, Send men to Joppa, and call for Simon, whose surname is Peter; who shall tell thee words, whereby thou and all thy house shall be saved. And as I began to speak, the Holy Ghost fell on them, as on us at the beginning. Then remembered I the word of the Lord, how that he said, John indeed baptized with water; but ye shall be baptized with the Holy Ghost."

The Apostle Paul, on his conversion to Christianity, had an encounter with the Lord Jesus Christ. As Paul was praying in the temple in Jerusalem, he fell into a trance vision. In this trance vision Paul saw the Lord Jesus. In this vision Jesus was instructing Paul to leave the city of Jerusalem in haste because the people would not believe his testimony, (Acts 22:17–21). *"And it came to pass, that, when I was come again to Jerusalem, even while I prayed in the temple, I was in a trance; and saw him saying unto me, Make haste, and get thee quickly out of Jerusalem: for they will not receive thy testimony concerning me. And I said, Lord, they know that I imprisoned and beat in every synagogue them that believed on thee: and when the blood of thy martyr Stephen was shed, I also was standing by, and consenting unto his death, and kept the raiment of them that slew him. And he said unto me, Depart: for I will send thee far hence unto the Gentiles."* Here we find again that Paul was awake when he had this trace vision.

Our third vision we will look at is *open* vision. On the mountain of transfiguration where Jesus took Peter, James, and John up into the mountain, we see a good example of what an open vision is. We can also say that Peter, James, and John were operating in the gift of discerning of spirits. An open vision is when someone is not sleeping and is not in a trance, but they are able to see in the spirit realm while they are wide awake and fully conscious of their immediate surroundings.

In this open vision encounter, Elijah and Moses appeared in the spirit along with Jesus. Matthew 17:1–9 gives the account: *"And after six days Jesus taketh Peter, James, and John his brother, and bringeth them up into an high mountain apart, and was transfigured before them: and his face did shine as the sun, and his raiment was white as the light. And, behold, there appeared unto them Moses and Elias talking with him. Then answered Peter, and said unto Jesus, Lord, it is good for us to be here: if thou wilt, let us make here three tabernacles; one for thee, and one for Moses, and one for Elias. While he yet spake, behold, a bright cloud overshadowed them: and behold a voice out of the cloud, which said, this is my beloved Son, in whom I am well pleased; hear ye him. And when the disciples heard it, they fell on their face, and were sore afraid. And Jesus came and touched them, and said, arise, and be not afraid. And when they had lifted up their eyes, they saw no man, save Jesus only. And as they came down from the mountain, Jesus charged them, saying, Tell the vision to no man, until the Son of man be risen again from the dead."*

The Apostle John, when he was on the Island of Patmos receiving the revelation message from Jesus Christ, had some opened visions. It is possible that most of the messages of the book of Revelation were open vision encounters that John had with Jesus Christ. *"I was in the Spirit on the Lord's day, and heard behind me* a great voice, as of a trumpet, saying, I am Alpha and Omega, the first and the last: and, What thou seest, write in a book, and send it unto the seven churches which are in Asia; unto Ephesus, and unto Smyrna, and unto Pergamos, and unto Thyatira, and unto Sardis, and unto Philadelphia, and unto Laodicea. And I turned to see the voice that spake with me. And being turned, I saw seven golden candlesticks; and in the midst of the seven candlesticks one like unto the Son of man, clothed with a garment down to the foot, and girt about the paps with a golden girdle. His head and his hairs were white like wool, as white as snow; and his eyes were as a flame of fire; and his feet like unto fine brass, as if they burned in a furnace; and his voice as the sound of many waters. And he had in his right hand seven stars: and out of his mouth went a sharp two-edged sword: and his countenance was as the sun shineth in his strength. And when I saw him, I fell at his feet as dead. And he laid his right hand upon me, saying unto me, Fear not; I am the first and the last: I am he that liveth, and was dead; and, behold, I am alive for evermore, Amen; and have the keys of hell and of death. Write the things which thou hast seen, and the things which are, and the *things which shall be hereafter; the mystery of the seven stars which thou sawest in my right hand, and the seven golden candlesticks. The seven stars are the angels of the seven churches: and the seven candlesticks which thou sawest are the seven churches. After this I looked, and, behold, a door was opened in heaven: and the first voice which I heard was as it were of a trumpet talking with me; which said, Come up hither, and I will shew thee things which must be hereafter"* (Revelation 1:10–20; 4:1).

We can understand through those few examples how visions come to us; dream, trance, and open. I experienced all three in my encounters. It is not significant that you understand how the visions came to me but that you focus on the messages they bring to us. I trust that as you glean through these pages you will be inspired to draw near to the Lord Jesus, because I believe this is the main purpose I was given these spiritual experiences that I will now share with you.

The Messenger

Rochester, New York will always remain a special place for me. Besides being born and raised in Rochester, I experienced there all my momentous divine encounters with the Lord Jesus and His creation. I was born to my parents in Rochester on January 2, 1941. We were a happy family. My dad was a tough Sicilian brick mason. He was rugged, but he was also a hardworking family man. My mother was a sweet woman who dearly loved her children. Today I realize how blessed and rich we were back then, because we had two parents who loved, cared for, and provided the best they could for me and my siblings.

I still remember Star Market, our local grocery chain, and I remember my school years

at St. Francis Xavier and East High School.
Youthful innocence was certainly more prevalent
then. My childhood was always characterized by
sibling rivals and juvenile feats and adventures.
Having visions of the afterlife, especially on the
negative side, was an incomprehensible prospect
for a youth back then. As you read further on,
you will discover that my boyish craving for
periodic doses of invincibility landed me in the
midst of my most notable heavenly experience.

As time went by, I grew up and had a family
of my own. My wife and I bore four children.
The Lord God granted us His blessing; we
have our quiver full with grandchildren. The
psalmist reminds us: *As arrows are in the hand
of a mighty man; so are children of the youth.
Happy is the man that hath his quiver full
of them: they shall not be ashamed, but they
shall speak with the enemies in the gate (Psalm
127:4–5).*

In my childhood years, I saw family as a
very important ingredient in my life. I always
loved to be around my family, especially around
the holiday seasons. I knew then that one day,
when I had grown up, I would have a wife
and children of my own. I once thought about
becoming a catholic priest. But, once I found out

that a priest was forbidden to marry and have children, I changed my mind about studying for the priesthood.

So far, our children have now delivered twelve offspring of their own. Much like any grandparent, I find my grandchildren are a delight. My wife and I are privileged to visit and care for these little ones, our heritage. Scripture says it correctly: *"Children are a heritage of the Lord and the fruit of the womb is His reward" (Psalm 127:3).* If you are a sane parent, you must know how precious children are. The Lord especially cherishes children. He speaks of the woe that awaits anyone who harms these little ones. The Lord also admonishes His church, telling us how that we are to become as little children in order for us to enter into His kingdom.

At the same time came the disciples unto Jesus, saying, Who is the greatest in the kingdom of heaven? And Jesus called a little child unto him, and set him in the midst of them, and said, Verily I say unto you, Except ye be converted, and become as little children, ye shall not enter into the kingdom of heaven. Whosoever therefore shall humble himself as this little child, the same is greatest in the kingdom of heaven. And whoso shall receive one such little child in my name receiveth me. But whoso shall offend one of these little ones which believe in me, it were better for him that a millstone were hanged about his neck, and that he were drowned in the depth of the sea (Matthew 18:1–6). Children are innocent and full of faith. They will believe mostly what they are told. It is this kind of faith that the Lord implores the Church to cultivate. You will benefit from this kind of faith as you harvest insights from the pages of this book.

God blessed our forefathers who did right in the sight of the Lord. When our forefathers walked in the fear of the Lord, it caused a domino effect of blessings to fall down upon us and upon our children's children. When our forefathers do evil it caused generational curse to be passed down to our children's children; even to the fourth generation. *"And the LORD passed by before him, and proclaimed, The LORD, The LORD God, merciful and gracious, longsuffering, and abundant in goodness and truth, keeping mercy for thousands, forgiving iniquity and transgression and sin, and that will by no means clear the guilty; visiting the iniquity of the fathers upon the children, and upon the children's children, unto the third and to the fourth generation" (Exodus 34:6-7).*

I can honestly say that I have a special crown in my life at this time. My children's children caused me to have this crown. I love my grandchildren very much because they remind me of my children when they were young. I can claim this crown of a grand dad according to King Solomon; the wisest man who ever lived. I am my children's glory and they may not even know it. *"Children's children are the crown of old men; and the glory of children are their fathers"* (Proverbs 17:6). God does use children and youth to get His message across.

I do not consider myself a prophet, neither do I conclude that visions from the Almighty necessarily makes one a prophet. Scripture tells us that a prophet is without honor in his own city and country. *"And they were offended in him. But Jesus said unto them, A prophet is not without honour, save in his own country, and in his own house"* (Matthew 13:57). It is much better for a Prophet to be endorsed by God Himself rather than by man. When a true Prophet inspired by the Holy Spirit prays we will get results. Sometimes if we interfere with a true Prophet of God, God Himself will deal with us. *"Now therefore restore the man his wife; for he is a prophet, and he shall pray for thee, and thou shalt live: and if thou restore her not, know thou that thou shalt surely die, thou, and all that are thine"* (Genesis 20:7).

We are warned by Jesus concerning false Prophets in the end-times. Because we are living in the end-times, we should be wise and discerning of those who claim that they are a Prophet of the Lord. Jesus said that we will know a true Prophet or a false Prophet by their fruit. Many false Prophets are coming on the scene and they are deceiving many good people. Scripture says *"And many false prophets shall rise, and shall deceive many"* (Matthew 24:11). Do not be impressed by the miracles, signs, and wonders that some of these Prophets perform. Yes, they may heal the sick and even cast out demons and preach the word, but in God's eyes they could be false Prophets. Scripture reminds us that *"There shall arise false Christs, and false prophets, and shall shew great signs and wonders; insomuch that, if it were possible, they shall deceive the very elect"* (Matthew 24:24).

According to some teachings, a true Prophet should operate or flow in two revelation gifts and one utterance gift. Looking back at what

Jesus said about the New Testament Prophet, He said that we will know a true Prophet of God by his fruit. True Prophets should bear good fruit. *"Beware of false prophets, which come to you in sheep's clothing, but inwardly they are ravening wolves. Ye shall know them by their fruits. Do men gather grapes of thorns, or figs of thistles? Even so every good tree bringeth forth good fruit; but a corrupt tree bringeth forth evil fruit. A good tree cannot bring forth evil fruit neither can a corrupt tree bring forth good fruit. Every tree that bringeth not forth good fruit is hewn down, and cast into the fire. Wherefore, by their fruits ye shall know them"* (Matthew 7:15–20).

Jesus was a true Prophet. His own siblings could not respect the office of a Prophet that He walked in. He prophesied His own death on the cross. So often our own household will be the last ones to recognize the call of God in our lives. Let us not be discouraged concerning this. If Jesus had a hard time with His brethren's acknowledgment of who He was, then we can expect similar treatment, as He reminded us. *"And he said, Verily I say unto you, No prophet is accepted in his own country"* (Luke 4:24). Sometimes we will be rejected by those who know us and even by our family members. Let us not be discouraged when friends and family do not acknowledge the anointing or gifts of God in our lives. Jesus Himself was not recognized by His family and neighbors to be the Son of God or even to be God Himself. The Scribes and Pharisees claimed that Jesus committed the sin of blasphemy. The sin of blasphemy was the sin that led to Jesus's death sentence on the cross of Calvary. His critics said, *"Is not this the carpenter's son? Is not His mother called Mary and His brethren, James, and Joses, and Simon, and Judas? And His sisters, are they not all with us? Whence then hath this man all these things? And they were offended in Him. But Jesus said unto them, A prophet is not without honour, save in his own country, and in his own house"* (Matthew 13:55–57).

There are times when a true man or woman of God prophesies or gives a word of prophecy to someone and the prophecy does not manifest the way one thinks it should. We should not be quick to judge that servant of God to be a false prophet or prophetess. Scripture tells us that *"we know in part and we prophesy in part"* (1 Corinthians 13:9). Visions are sometimes symbolic of people, place, time, and object.

We see this happen in the dream of Joseph in Genesis. We see that the seven favored cows represented seven years, and the seven good nourished ears of corn represented seven years as well. *"And it came to pass at the end of two full years that Pharaoh dreamed: and, behold, he stood by the river. And, behold, there came up out of the river seven well favoured kine and fatfleshed; and they fed in a meadow. And, behold, seven other kine came up after them out of the river, ill favoured and leanfleshed; and stood by the other kine upon the brink of the river. And the ill favoured and leanfleshed kine did eat up the seven well favoured and fat kine. So Pharaoh awoke. And he slept and dreamed the second time: and, behold, seven ears of corn came up upon one stalk, rank and good. And, behold seven thin ears and blasted with the east wind sprung up after them. And the seven thin ears devoured the seven rank and full ears. And Pharaoh awoke, and, behold, it was a dream"* (Genesis 41:1-7).

Visions are not always interpreted or fulfilled in the way our human minds comprehend them, so we must receive them by faith and leave the performing of them to the Lord. In accordance, you can be sure that, I am committed to reporting, in whole, a true account of what was delivered to me by the Lord Himself. My writing to you also requires a measure of faith on my part, so I trust you will be thoroughly persuaded to the degree that you prepare yourself for what is ahead of us all. I am God's messenger, and I give His message to you.

Why would the Almighty sometimes give visions to the young as was the case with me? Scripture tells us that His young men would see visions. In scripture, God used many of His servants at an early age. Let us be opened to what the Holy Spirit is doing in these last days. We are in the season where the Spirit of the Lord is moving upon some of the most unlikely people. God said that He will use the foolish things of the world to confound the wise. There is going to be a great outpouring of the Holy Spirit upon the earth like never before. This will bring in the greatest harvest of souls just before the Rapture of the Church of Jesus Christ. In this coming end-time revival, we are going to see young men and young women operating in the gifts of prophesy, and older mature men will have more dreams than before. More and more young men will see visions. Some young men will have open visions. Some young men will have trance visions. There will be an outpouring of God's Spirit upon God's servants; male and female. Joel 2:28–29 states, *"And it shall come to pass afterward, that I will pour out my spirit upon all flesh; and your sons and your daughters shall prophesy, your old men shall dream dreams, your young men shall see visions: and also upon the servants and upon the handmaids in those days will I pour out my spirit."*

Some visions will not be symbolic but they will be straightforward. King Solomon had a straightforward vision in the early part of his reign. *"In Gibeon the LORD appeared to Solomon in a dream by night: and God said, Ask what I shall give thee. And Solomon said, Thou hast shewed unto thy servant David my father great mercy, according as he walked before thee in truth, and in righteousness, and in uprightness of heart with thee; and thou hast kept for him this great kindness, that thou hast given him a son to sit on his throne, as it is this day. And now, O LORD my God, thou hast made thy servant king instead of David my father: and I am but a little child: I know not how to go out or come in. And thy servant is in the midst of thy people which thou hast chosen, a great people, that cannot be numbered nor counted for multitude. Give therefore thy servant an understanding heart to judge thy people that I may discern between good and bad: for who is able to judge this thy so great a people? And the speech pleased the LORD, that Solomon had asked this thing. And God said unto him, Because thou hast asked this thing, and hast not asked for thyself long life; neither hast asked riches for thyself, nor hast asked the life of thine enemies; but hast asked for thyself understanding to discern judgment; behold, I have done according to thy words: lo, I have given thee a wise and an understanding heart; so that there was none like thee before thee, neither after thee shall any arise like unto thee. And I have also given thee that which thou hast not asked, both riches, and honour: so that there shall not be any among the kings like unto thee all thy days. And if thou wilt walk in my ways, to keep my statutes and my commandments, as thy father David did walk, then I will lengthen thy days. And Solomon awoke; and, behold, it was a dream. And he came to Jerusalem, and stood before the ark of the covenant of the LORD, and offered up burnt offerings, and offered peace offerings, and made a feast to all his servants"* (1 Kings 3:1–15).

I received the Lord Jesus into my life at the age of 9. My mother was the channel through which the gospel of Christ came to me. Though she was not a practicing Christian then, but she would teach me the way of the Lord. It was at this early age that Jesus, by His Holy Spirit, revealed to me that every sickness and disease has an evil spirit associated with it. So, when you pray for someone, you should pray against the spirit of the pertinent infirmity. Cancer, heart attack, diabetes, stroke; any sickness or disease known to man did not come from our Lord Jesus. Spirits of sickness and diseases, spirits of oppression, spirits of witchcraft: these are spirits of infirmity and they are from Satan himself. All the things that hinder the human body from functioning well, and eventually causing it to die, came upon humanity from the curse originated in the Garden of Eden. Our fore parents Adam and Eve were deceived by Satan in the Garden. Sickness and diseases came upon the human family by Satan and his demons. Every sickness and disease came upon the human race by demonic spirits. Some of these sickness and diseases were passed down from generation to generation. This is called generational curse. Medical science calls it genetics.

Sicknesses will not be cured by medicine or physical therapy if they are a direct result of demonic encounters. It will take supernatural healing by the Holy Spirit. The woman who had the spirit of infirmity for eighteen years could only be healed by the supernatural power of Jesus Christ. *"And, behold, there was a woman which had a spirit of infirmity eighteen years, and was bowed together, and could in no wise lift up herself. And when Jesus saw her, he called her to him, and said unto her, Woman, thou art loosed from thine infirmity. And he laid his hands on her: and immediately she was made straight, and glorified God"* (Luke 13:11–13).

Jesus died that we would be set free from sickness and diseases. He received stripes that we would be healed. *"Surely he hath borne our griefs, and carried our sorrows: yet we did esteem him stricken, smitten of God, and afflicted. But he was wounded for our transgressions, He was bruised for our iniquities: the chastisement of our peace was upon him; and with His stripes we are healed"* (Isaiah 53:4–5). When someone is sick and his or her doctor, through medical science, cannot figure out the sickness, in most cases there is a demon behind that sickness or disease. Jesus Christ came into the world to be a symbolic act for our healing. Healing and deliverance are part of our salvation package. When a person accepts Jesus Christ as Savior and Lord, he or she has legal rights to supernatural healing and deliverance by faith in Jesus's name. Because of Adam's sin of disobedience, the human race inherited sickness and diseases. Jesus Christ came into the world for our salvation.

It is amazing to know that Isaiah the Prophet, who began his ministry about 740 B.C., accurately prophesied Christ's suffering on the cross. Christ Jesus suffered much intense pain for our transgressions. He did this in exchange for our healing. The crown of thorns was upon His head and it pierced His skull. Blood flowed from Jesus's head down to His forehead and some into His eyes. They chastised Him with a whip that carried sharp objects that would tear into His flesh. These were sharp glass and metal hooks that would rip the flesh from His body. Blood flowed from Jesus's broken body. The stripes that He received on His back were an exchange for our healing. That is how much

God loves us. When we pray for healing, we can pray Isaiah 53:5 and claim our healing by faith in Jesus's name.

At the age of 15 all my interests were in the arena of baseball cards and girls. I loved the Lord but I had my moments of distraction. God, however, had a much better plan for my life. In many cases, it is often difficult to capture the attention of teens when it comes to faithful commitment to the things of God. The Lord was able to apprehend me long enough to ask me to write Him a book. He simply said to me, "Lu, I want you to write a book". I told Him I could not. The Lord did not argue with me at this age but He did respond to my refusal. He said, "All right, I'll get somebody else to do it". This book was The Late Great Planet Earth written by Hal Lindsey. That book ministered to multitudes and sold millions. I could have retired on one book. I am not after money; far be it from me, but I am saying that if God ever asks you to do something, say 'yes' immediately. God did not insist on or try to persuade my obedience to Him, because He wanted to teach me a life lesson. He does not depend on our abilities to do what He tells us to do. He will give you what you need to do His will. I thought of myself as not having the qualifications to write a book, but God had the help I needed. If the Lord ever asks you to do something, say 'yes' immediately, and do not hesitate to do it in His time. If you are hanging on a cliff by one rope and He says "let go", let go and you'll learn how to fly. In the proceeding chapters I will share with you in detail what the Lord showed me through visions.

The nation of the United States of America is a large part of God's revelation to me and now to you as well. Truly it is needful that the Lord shorten man's days in this earth, otherwise no flesh will be saved. *"For then shall be great tribulation, such as was not since the beginning of the world to this time, no, nor ever shall be. And except those days should be shortened, there should no flesh be saved: but for the elect's sake those days shall be shortened"* (Matthew 24:21–22).

As the world draws closer to the end of this age or dispensation, we need to take a closer look at the Middle East. Iran is trying to take the military lead with Russia; taking a stand with them as one of their allies. Iran's nuclear program is a great threat to Israel, to America, and to the rest of the Western World.

If there would be a nuclear war with Russia from the North, Iran and Israel in the Middle East, and America in the West, it would cause a worldwide catastrophe as was never seen in the history of humanity. I am not quite sure what role America will play after the rapture of the Church. According to Bible Prophesy, there will be a seven year tribulation period upon the earth. The first half of the seven years tribulation will not be good, but it will be tolerable in comparison to the second half. The second half of the tribulation is called "The Time of Jacob's Trouble" (Jeremiah 30:7). *"Alas! for that day is great, so that none is like it: it is even the time of Jacob's trouble, but he shall be saved out of it."* The second half of the tribulation period is also referred to as "Great Tribulation" (Matthew 24:21).

This great nation of the United States is largely hated by other prominent nations because of its world dominance. Envy is the root cause of America's prominent enemies, and they will passionately and relentlessly pursue this great nation by means of deception. The Lord God is sending forth warnings to America through His servants in hopes that she will awake and turn to the Living God.

The Lord also granted me visions of hell, the lake of fire, and Satan himself. Many people do not believe there is such a thing as hell or even demons. They are sadly mistaken. The truth is, the world beyond this world is much more a reality. What we can see is only for a short span of time, but what we cannot see is for eternity. *"For now we see through a glass, darkly; but then face to face: now I know in part; but then shall I know even as also I am known"* (1 Corinthians 13:12). The seen or known world is slave to the unseen or unknown world. The spiritual world dominates and is superior to the natural world. These truths do not require man's belief; they stand indisputable and independent of man's approval or understanding.

There is an invisible world around us that we can only see with our spiritual eyes. The natural or naked eye cannot see it. Someone might say that he does not believe that there is a God because he cannot see Him. He does not believe in what he cannot see. I would challenge that person concerning the wind that causes great hurricanes that leaves destruction and damage to our towns and communities. We cannot see the wind but it is real because we see the effects of it. So is it with God; we do not see Him because He is a Spirit, but we certainly see the works of His hands. *"The heavens declare the glory of God; and the firmament sheweth His handywork"* (Psalm 19:1). How about electricity? We cannot see it with our eyes but we respect the power of it. We also see the power of the wireless cell phones how it works by the technologies of satellite. The invisible spirit world is very real, and that is where God, as a Spirit, rules. *"While we look not at the things which are seen, but at the things which are not seen: for the things which are seen are temporal; but the things which are not seen are eternal"* (2 Corinthians 4:18).

If one understands the realms of the underground world, no one in his sound mind would want to go to hell. No one would even dare to wish his worst enemy such eternal demise. Scripture makes descriptive mention of the lake of fire, and what I saw was nothing short of that expression. *"But the fearful, and unbelieving, and the abominable, and murderers, and whoremongers, and sorcerers, and idolaters, and all liars, shall have their part in the lake which burneth with fire and brimstone: which is the second death"* (Revelation 21:8). *"And the beast was taken, and with him the false prophet that wrought miracles before him, with which he deceived them that had received the mark of the beast, and them that worshipped his image. These both were cast alive into a lake of fire burning with brimstone"* (Revelation 19:20). *"And the devil that deceived them was cast into the lake of fire and brimstone, where the beast and the false prophet are, and shall be tormented day and night for ever and ever"* (Revelation 20:10). A dear friend once asked me what the lake of fire was like. I told him that it was just like looking at one of the five great lakes that separates the US and Canada. It was like viewing Lake Ontario, only it was a great lake that looks like an ocean filled with flaming fires. I even smelled sulfur coming from the lake. God let me see the lake of fire as real as it was. According to scriptures, the Lake of Fire would be like eternal prison for everyone whose name was not written in the Book of Life. Hell is like a jail where people who died without Christ would stay and wait for Jesus Christ to judge them on that Day of Judgment. The souls in hell will be judged and sentenced for eternity to the Lake of Fire. *"And the devil that deceived them was cast into the lake of fire and brimstone, where the beast and the false prophet are, and shall be tormented day and night for ever and ever. And death and hell were cast into the lake of fire. This is the second death. And whosoever was not found written in the book of life was cast into the lake of fire"* (Revelation 20:10, 14–15).

Hell was not created for man. Scripture tells us that hell was created for the Devil and his angels. Some people do not believe there is a place called hell. The Bible clearly states that hell is a real place. God made hell for Satan and his angels who rebelled against God. When Satan rebelled against God Almighty, God sentenced him to the lower part of the pit of hell. *"For thou hast said in thine heart, I will ascend into heaven, I will exalt my throne above the stars of God: I will sit also upon the mount of the congregation, in the sides of the north: I will ascend above the heights of the clouds; I will be like the most High. Yet thou shalt be brought down to hell, to the sides of the pit"* (Isaiah 14:13–15).

I heard an ex-coworker once say that he did not want to go to heaven because he cannot drink beer and party with his friends. This co-worker also said that he'd rather go to hell where he can party with friends. But in reality, hell is a place of sorrow, suffering, loneliness, and torment. *"The sorrows of hell compassed me about; the snares of death prevented me"* (2 Samuel 22:6). *"Then shall he say also unto them on the left hand, Depart from me, ye cursed, into everlasting fire, prepared for the devil and his angels"* (Matthew 25:41). What the Lord showed me of that eternal damnation clearly portrays its original purpose. Hell was not made for mankind. Hell is a terrible place.

Satan is the master of disguise and deception. He will drag souls who are unyielding to Christ down with him to an eternity without Christ. Satan is not as man imagines him to be; a mankind dressed in red attire, having two horns and a pitch fork. Contrary to popular beliefs, even among evangelical Christians, Satan has power and is too strong for those who are not in Christ. Our power to conquer the Devil is found only in Christ. He gives us the authority to trample over all the power of the enemy and not be harmed (Luke 10:19).

It is vitally important that man understands that Satan hates him. Satan is not a friend of man as some are deceived in believing. His main hold on man is deception, and that was how he overthrew man in the Garden of Eden. *"Now the serpent was more subtil than any beast of the field which the LORD God had made. And he said unto the woman, Yea, hath God said, Ye shall not eat of every tree of the garden?"* (Genesis 3:1). Mankind, without the indwelling of the Holy Spirit, is no match for the devil. Peter, before his baptism with the Holy Spirit on the Day of Pentecost, was trying to influence Jesus to not go to the cross. Jesus's main purpose for coming to planet earth was to die on the cross for humanity. Satan, working within Jesus's inner circle through Peter, was trying to stop Jesus from His main mission. *"From that time forth began Jesus to shew unto his disciples, how that he must go unto Jerusalem, and suffer many things of the elders and chief priests and scribes, and be killed, and be raised again the third day. Then Peter took him, and began to rebuke him, saying, be it far from thee, Lord: this shall not be unto thee. But he turned, and said unto Peter, Get thee behind me, Satan: thou art an offence unto me: for thou savourest not the things that be of God, but those that be of men"* (Matthew 16:21–23). The Devil is also a spirit; therefore, because he is not seen with natural eyes, his power to deceive and conquer is magnified.

I also received a glimpse into God's heaven. Heaven is a beautiful place. There are rules to reaching that heavenly plateau. Heaven is nothing man can ever imagine or mimic. It is truly, as Abraham said, *"a city which hath foundations whose Builder and Maker is God"* (Hebrews 11:10). When you see heaven you will understand even more how much our heavenly Father loves humanity. He has prepared heaven for all mankind; whosoever will believe in His Son Jesus Christ. In my visions I also saw Jesus. In my heart and mind Jesus is who makes heaven shine. *"And the city had no need of the sun, neither of the moon, to shine in it: for the glory of God did lighten it, and the Lamb is the light thereof"* (Revelation 21:23). Jesus is largely misunderstood by much of humanity. He is not who many perceive Him to be; intrusive, unreachable, mystical, and some even dare to think Him to be weak.

As you glean through these faithful pages, you will discover the real Jesus. You will better understand His humanity and you will appreciate His deity. *"In the beginning was the Word, and the Word was with God, and the Word was God. And the Word was made flesh, and dwelt among us, (and we beheld his glory, the glory as of the only begotten of the Father,) full of grace and truth"* (John 1:1, 14). Everyone have a different concept of what heaven is. Most, if not all people, want to go to the heaven they imagine. Fortunately for humanity, heaven is not left up to our imaginations. Heaven is what God has made it, and approved citizenship is a must for eternal residence. The way to heaven is not a mystery. God has made it easy for man since heaven was made for man's eternal dwelling. He has given us His Son, Jesus Christ; the Way, the Truth, and the Life. *"Jesus saith unto him, I am the way, the truth, and the life: no man cometh unto the Father, but by me"* (John 14:6). Are you prepared to enter heaven? Let us take a glance into what awaits us in God's heaven.

From Time Into Eternity

At the age of 21, in the year 1962, my whole perception of and appreciation for God and His Kingdom took a drastic turn. At the Park Avenue Hospital in Rochester, I underwent a surgery on my nose that sustained damages from an accident that occurred during my childhood. This accident occurred while I was out leisurely riding my bicycle and had a moment of inspiration that lured me to do something a little different. The thought came to me that if I could handle this bike in such a way that would somewhat cause me to soar above ground, that would be awesome. That boyish irresponsible nature I mentioned earlier was my master; I submitted to the urge to fly. My actions fostered the event of the accident that landed me on a concrete pavement where I collided with a tree stump that protruded. The impact broke my nose. Over time my nostrils grew distorted to the point where I had difficulty breathing.

Now age 21, I was taken to the hospital where an operation was performed on my nostrils. Both air passages of my nostrils were blocked up by the bone on the inside being deformed from the accident. Before surgery, I was given twilight drug to put me out for the operation; however, an overdose was administered. The surgeons chiseled the bone out and opened up my air passages. During the procedure my heart stopped while I laid there on the operating table. I experienced death.

My spirit left my body, and I was now above the room looking down on myself and the two doctors who were working on me. I remember having no concern or care of what was occurring. On my conversion to Christ at age 9, I had made a commitment to God that, unto death if necessary, nothing would move me from Him. I was never one to indulge in strong drinks or alcohol. I've had an occasional shot of whisky to warm up my bones while shoveling the driveway in deep winter months. The relaxed feeling that one experiences when alcohol is in the body was how I felt while the surgeons worked fervently to resuscitate my body.

My spirit soared above and through the roof of the hospital. Now I am above the earth looking on it as it now appears to be just a swirly blue marble. I experienced speed beyond anything man can ever do or imagine. The planets were going by me at lightning speed. It all looked like a white picket fence for the speed. In a moment's time I entered a tunnel. It was a black walled tunnel, but I could see through it as it were of transparent thick glass. At the end of the tunnel was a great light.

Reaching the end of the tunnel my focus was fixed on this great light. For a brief moment I looked away and down at my feet and discovered that I was standing on rectangular shaped gold tiles. I could see the beauty of heaven that makes one joyful, and there were also stars twinkling under my feet. This went on as far as I could see because the tiles too were transparent. If I had eyesight to see across Kansas, that's how vast it looked to me. This was just the foyer; the entrance way to God's heaven.

I reset my focus on the huge light at the tunnel's exit. It was the kind of light that did not hurt my eyes. I gazed steadfastly at this light, and from it I sensed awesome power, love, authority, and an acceptance of me just the way I was. I began communicating with the light through thought exchanges. I asked the light "are you God?" The reply was, "yes". Scripture tells us that *"God is light, and in Him is no darkness at all"* (1 John 1:5). I asked God if I could see what He looked like behind the light. God's image appeared behind the light in a magnified form. At this point, the radiance of His light disappeared. My eyes were different there than they are here. The Almighty seemed to be approximately 100 yards away from me yet I could see Him up close. The stature of this superior being looked like the figure of a man. Human beings were created in God's image. *"So God created man in his own image, in the image of God created he him; male and female created he them"* (Genesis 1:27). We also know that God the Father and Jesus Christ the Son are one. *"Jesus saith unto him, have I been so long time with you, and yet hast thou not known me, Philip? He that hath seen me hath seen the Father; and how sayest thou then, Shew us the Father?"* (John 14:9).

Satan has deceived a great percentage of humanity in believing that Jesus Christ could not be God or the Son of God. The Devil caused many to believe that because Jesus came in the form of a man; a humble man, He could not be God because God should be some great big being somewhere in the universe. Man was created in the image of God. It makes a lot of sense that man would look like God and God would look like man. Jesus Christ was God manifested in the flesh so that God could communicate with man on a one on one level. *"Beware lest any man spoil you through philosophy and vain deceit, after the tradition of men, after the rudiments of the world, and not after Christ. For in him dwelleth all the fullness of the Godhead bodily"* (Colossians 2:8–9).

I believe that God can manifest Himself to be whatever He chooses. With God anything is possible. He can be spirit and He can be natural. He can be vast and He can be small. God is able to be transfigured. *"And after six days Jesus taketh with him Peter, and James, and John, and leadeth them up into an high mountain apart by themselves: and he was transfigured before them"* (Mark 9:2). I do not believe He necessarily appears to everyone the same way in every experience. He is unpredictable and cannot be assumed upon or understood by man.

He is past finding out and that's a part of the reason why He is God. *"O the depth of the riches both of the wisdom and knowledge of God! How unsearchable are his judgments, and his ways past finding out!"* (Romans 11:33).

In my experience, God was approximately 6 feet in height and about 190 pounds. He had close trimmed beard, shoulder length hair, and a white robe to the ankle with full length sleeves. The Almighty was very beautiful, not handsome. This was the Lord Jesus.

I am now communicating face to face with Jesus Christ. I had three questions I desperately wanted to ask Him. To these three questions He gave me three answers. My first question to the Lord was concerning my family's salvation. My folks were not church going people neither had they, from my observation, any relationship with the Lord, so I was troubled about their eternal wellbeing. To my first question the Lord said to me simply, "They will all accept Me". Salvation is not about God accepting us, but it is about us sinners accepting His sacrifice. *"For God so loved the world, that he gave his only begotten Son, that whosoever believeth in him should not perish, but have everlasting life"* (John 3:16). Father God took Someone who was beautiful, lovely, clean and perfect and He made Him dirt for us. Sin was put on Jesus Christ when He came to earth for us.

In 1986 at a little Pentecostal Church called Four Square, located behind the international airport in Rochester, my parents, my sister, and my brother all had a born-again experience. When the Spirit of the Lord came upon the congregation, my father stood shaking uncontrollably and my mother was seated shaking likewise under the power of Almighty God. God showed them He was real. My sister and brother were laid out on the floor and were not able to get up for a while. They were speaking in a language they never learned. There were 5 conversions from my home and these included my brother's fiancée. This all happened eight days after my meeting with the Lord. This was a true household salvation. *"And they said, believe on the Lord Jesus Christ, and thou shalt be saved, and thy house"* (Acts 16:31).

The second question I asked the Lord was concerning what time suffering and pain would cease for mankind. As a young man I was already exhausted with the dilemma of humanity; sicknesses, diseases, civil rivals, addictions, depravity, and family dysfunction were rampant. In answer to my second question, the Lord spoke these exact words to me: "In your time; your generation; you will see it with your own eyes". I am now seventy one years old so I recon we do not have a whole lot of time left. The Holy Bible informs us that the generation that witnesses the rebirth of Israel as a nation will witness the return of the Lord. We are that generation. The Lord is coming to clean up the earth and to rule it.

The Lord's answer to the third and last question I asked Him still bothers me today. I asked the Lord how many people will go to be with Him when He returns. He used a percentage to answer me. I realize that there are many varied understanding as it pertains to the number of people who will attain to the heavenly Kingdom. Many numbers and percentages are floating around. I can only give you what God gave to me. The interpretation and understanding I leave with God. Scripture reminds us that *"we know in part and we prophesy in part"* (1 Corinthians 13:9). The Lord said, "The percentage of humanity that will escape hell is 12 percent". Is this hell referring to the state of earth after the rapture of the church but before the millennium? Is it referring to the literal hell of eternal separation from God and damnation with unquenchable fire? Whatever the interpretation, 12 percent does not say too much for us, does it?

Concerning entrance into God's marriage supper, in scripture we understand that there were ten virgins called to the event. Five of these virgins were wise and five were foolish. The foolish were denied entrance because they were not ready. *"And while they went to buy, the bridegroom came; and they that were ready went in with him to the marriage: and the door was shut. Afterward came also the other virgins, saying, Lord, Lord, open to us. But he answered and said, Verily I say unto you, I know you not. Watch therefore, for ye know neither the day nor the hour wherein the Son of man cometh"* (Matthew 25:10–13). Since they were virgins, this group of ten, where only 50 percent were accepted, could be in reference to the church. Whatever the interpretations, it sufficeth to say, God's message to us is that we be ready for His coming. The low percentages are frightening and astounding to me, but His word also speaks of an innumerable multitude of people who will enter in at the final call after the great tribulation. *"After this I beheld, and, lo, a great multitude, which no man could number, of all nations, and kindreds, and people, and tongues, stood before the throne, and before the Lamb, clothed with white robes, and palms in their hands. And I said unto him, Sir, thou knowest. And he said to me, these are they which came out of great tribulation, and have washed their robes, and made them white in the blood of the Lamb"* (Revelation 7:9, 14).

This generation speaks of God as though He was conformed to whoever or whatever they imagine or choose to believe. God is not subject to man's understanding or perception, and that is why He is God. Everyone seems to have his own god. The god that most people worship today is exchangeable; it can be stuffed in my pocket; it can increase or decrease in value; it is controlled by man; it is money. Money is God to most of humanity including those who claim to be Christians. In the eyes of the Lord, money is like toilet paper, and people go crazy to hang on to toilet paper and they will do anything to get it. *"For the love of money is the root of all evil: which while some coveted after, they have erred from the faith, and pierced themselves through with many sorrows"* (1Timothy 6:10).

Who or what is your God today? Do not read this book as just another interesting story of the unseen worlds. It is written as God's warning to all of us. It is time for us to take inventory of our lives and make a decision concerning where we plan to spend eternity. Time is very short dear reader. Even if you live a hundred years, that's only a drop in the ocean of eternity's span. Are you part of the five wise virgins? If not, why not today? The Bible is profitable for all and was written for doctrine, reproof, correction, instruction in righteousness. (2 Timothy 3:16). God, by His Holy Spirit, inspired holy men to write His word, and He is still writing inspiring words to us today. The heeding is for us to do. Today is as good a day as any to be sure of our eternity. We insure everything else; automobile, mortal life, home. Why not insure your most precious possession? Why not insure your eternal soul?

The Lord also showed me that the big bang theory is true, and this is how He showed it to me. First there was total darkness, and then I sensed a whirling motion, and then it got bigger and bigger and seemingly compacted and then there was light. This light got white hot and then exploded. In the universe today all the planets are still going away from each other. But there will come a time according to scripture that all will enfold again. *"And the stars of heaven fell unto the earth, even as a fig tree casteth her untimely figs, when she is shaken of a mighty wind. And the heaven departed as a scroll when it is rolled together; and every mountain and island were moved out of their places. And the kings of the earth, and the great men, and the rich men, and the chief captains, and the mighty men, and every bondman, and every free man, hid themselves in the dens and in the rocks of the mountains"* (Revelation 6:13–15). The earth is going to come back upon itself like a scroll and then blow up again. The Lord is going to make a new creation; a new heaven and a new earth. So the big bang theory is true, but God is the One who orchestrated it. The Lord created the galaxies and the whole universe. He made all that we see and do not see. Out of nothing He made mass and gas and compressed them and blew them up into what man calls the big bang. Now all these planets are still expanding from the initial explosion. God is awesome. We need not struggle in our puny finite minds to figure Him out, because we'll never understand Him. We only need to accept and trust Him. It was all here when we arrived and it will all be here when we leave.

In the next chapter I will describe heaven to you the way it was revealed to me. My tour of heaven occurred at a different time from my experience of entering through the vale I previously described.

The Lord sent me back from His home and I awoke in the intensive care unit at Park Avenue Hospital. My mouth was parched and I looked over to the table beside my bed and there was a glass of water awaiting me. I reached out for the water and I remember my hand shaking from being so feeble. When I touched the glass I knocked it over and my nurse came running. I asked, "Could I have some water please?" After receiving water I was wheeled back to my room. I soon discovered a hole was in my chest; inserted there where the doctors worked to revive me. The Lord told me, "It's not time for you to be here; go back because I have work for you to do". I am doing His work now by delivering His message to whoever will listen and take heed. I did not want to come back to earth because, judging from the little I saw in the corridors of heaven's entrance, I imagine that heaven must be a beautiful place.

Heaven Is A Beautiful Place

In this chapter I will describe heaven the way it was shown me. Many writers have published their own record of what heaven looks like as it was revealed to them. If you are a reader who closely follows prophesy and visions of the unknown worlds, you will find many similarities in the true accounts of that heavenly Kingdom. It is important for you to understand that heaven is not revealed to every writer in the same capacity or scope.

Many people do not believe in a literal place called heaven. Some believe heaven will be a boring place with baby angels floating on clouds and playing on harps. The Bible, the word of the living God, has much to say about heaven.

Heaven is a place that is indescribable to the human mind. The walls and foundational structures of the city of heaven are made of precious stones like jasper. The city is made of pure crystal clear gold. The twelve gates of the city are made of twelve gigantic pearls. The streets of heaven are not made with asphalt as our streets are. Heaven's streets are made with pure crystal transparent gold, and it is made by God Himself. *"For he looked for a city which hath foundations, whose builder and maker is God"* (Hebrew 11:10).

I've been invited to God's heaven on three different occasions. One of the three journeys I outlined in chapter 2, and it describes my entrance on the threshold of heaven. In this chapter I will combine my other two journeys in describing the heaven I was made to see. I was in my teen years when I entered this glorious place called heaven. The night that changed my whole outlook on life as it pertains to time and eternity began with a visitation from an angelic being who came into my bedroom. He began with the salutation, "Fear not". I am not one to fear anything and so I had no fear. I was however very surprised, and pleasantly so. The angel said, "Come with me, the Lord wants you to see something". The next thing I knew was that we were in the atmosphere over the earth. For whatever reason, we got in a vehicle; there was no rocking and there were no motors. This vehicle was shaped like an egg; like World War II canopy and it closed us in. The angel was in a seat behind me and I was in the front.

When you travel by the spirit time and space are irrelevant. In scripture, Acts 8:39–40 gives an account of Philip, the Evangelist who was translated from one point to another after he expounded the word of God to a new believer. *"And when they were come up out of the water, the Spirit of the Lord caught away Philip, that the eunuch saw him no more: and he went on his way rejoicing. But Philip was found at Azotus: and passing through he preached in all the cities, till he came to Caesarea."* We call Philip's experience a translation or a quick transportation from one location to another in a timeframe that is humanly impossible.

As the angel and I made our travel through space, I beheld a room that had chairs occupied by demons. These demons were dressed like the ancient soldiers of Greece and Rome; brass, spear, and army arrays. They were having a great time laughing at man. We went passed them. The Bible tells us that we wrestle *"against principalities, against powers, against the rulers of the darkness of this world, against spiritual wickedness in high places"* (Ephesians 6:12). I was not afraid of these evil ones.

By the grace of the Lord I do not deal with fear. I believe it is because I do not fear dying. I've come up against demonic encounters many times but I am not careful for my life. I am ready to be offered up for the cause of Christ. If I must face evil for Christ's sake I count it an honor. My life is in the Lord's hands. He said if we are willing to lose our lives for His sake; in whatever capacity, we will find life (Matthew 16:25). The Bible also tells us that *"perfect love casteth out fear"* (1 John 4:18). When we understand how much we are loved by God who is love, we rest in Him, and when we rest fear is extinguished.

As we approached God's heaven, I realized that heaven is a planet much like earth. Earth is approximately 25,000 miles in circumference and heaven is 1,000,000. This is knowledge I receive as I make my journey with the angel. In God's heavenly realm, revelation and knowledge often comes nonverbally. The signals are often spiritual. Comparing earth's size to that of heaven is like sitting a beach ball beside a marble. Heaven looks the same as earth but there is no corruption.

We got to heaven in a short time; seemed like about 90 seconds. Once we got there we began walking up a path; a gravel type path that led up to the City of God. Nothing decays in heaven. There were neither wilted leaves nor wilted flowers; everything is prime, fresh, and clean. I saw a leaf fall off a tree and as it hits the grass it was absorbed. There is a lot to see when you first catch a glimpse of heaven, but the Lord allowed me to focus only on the things He wanted me to report. The air was filled with the smell of roses. There was beautiful music in the air; I could hear it throughout my tour. I saw animals. There are grass, trees, brooks, and springs of waters. I saw cats, dogs, squirrels, rabbits, horses, and birds. I saw pets I had as a boy; they were there. I do not fully comprehend that. It is my understanding that at death the soul of the beast returns to the ground and the soul of man returns to God. However, perhaps the Lord will grant us animal lovers like-pets as we once had on earth. That was not clear to me, but a measure of hope was given to me to see a childhood memory.

I am sure the Lord did not reveal His entire plan and purposes in scripture. He gave man just enough information to make the journey from earth to his eternal destiny. Anything is possible with God (Mark 10:27).

At one instant the Lord was my escort. I was walking up a gravel path with the Lord and we entered a barn with stalls. In the stalls were no animals, but instead there were arms, legs, eyeballs and various body parts. I said, "Lord, what is all this?" He said, "These are for my people but they do not ask for them". We as Americans depend too much on our medical coverage and not on God. We do not extend our faith enough to receive God's miracles that are in store for us. People in third world countries see far more miracles of healing than we do because they do not have insurance. They cannot depend on man, so they depend on God. I do not believe that body parts are physically displayed in heaven and sent down to earth in tangible natural form to people who have the faith to believe for them. I believe these body parts are there as a spiritual token and reminder of what God will do in healing His people on earth if they will believe for that healing.

Concerning your prayers; you can call on God to overthrow Satan and the demons and to put whatever disease you want to put on them as they did to us. You have the authority to do that. God does not listen to your words unless they join the intent of your heart. If you are not focused on the prayers you make unto God; being distracted in your thoughts while you pray, God does not listen. If your mouth is saying something and your heart is thinking something else, forget it, you are wasting your time. With God there are just two kinds of people; those who belong to the Lord and those who do not. Those who belong to God will dwell with Him, those who do not belong to God will not see Him, but they will dwell in outer darkness forever. In heaven there are no Italians, Africans, Caucasians, Indians, Hispanics, Asians, and so on. God calls all people His children.

In heaven there will be prizes and surprises. Revelation 21:9–23; 22:1–5 gives us a very brief picture of this place called heaven. *"And there came unto me one of the seven angels which had the seven vials full of the seven last plagues, and talked with me, saying, Come hither, I will shew thee the bride, the Lamb's wife. And he carried me away in the spirit to a great and high mountain, and shewed me that great city, the holy Jerusalem, descending out of heaven from God, having the glory of God: and her light was like unto a stone most precious, even like a jasper stone, clear as crystal; And had a wall great and high, and had twelve gates, and at the gates twelve angels, and names written thereon, which are the names of the twelve tribes of the children of Israel: On the east three gates; on the north three gates; on the south three gates; and on the west three gates. And the wall of the city had twelve foundations, and in them the names of the twelve apostles of the Lamb. And he that talked with me had a golden reed to measure the city, and the gates thereof, and the wall thereof. And the city lieth foursquare, and the length is as large as the breadth: and he measured the city with the reed, twelve thousand furlongs. The length and the breadth and the height of it are equal. And he measured the wall thereof, an hundred and forty and four cubits, according to the measure of a man, that is, of the angel. And the building of the wall of it was of jasper: and the city was pure gold, like unto clear glass. And the foundations of the wall of the city were garnished with all manner of precious stones.*

The first foundation was jasper; the second, sapphire; the third, a chalcedony; the fourth, an emerald; the fifth, sardonyx; the sixth, sardius; the seventh, chrysolyte; the eighth, beryl; the ninth, a topaz; the tenth, a chrysoprasus; the eleventh, a jacinth; the twelfth, an amethyst. And the twelve gates were twelve pearls: every several gate was of one pearl: and the street of the city was pure gold, as it were transparent glass. And I saw no temple therein: for the Lord God Almighty and the Lamb are the temple of it. And the city had no need of the sun, neither of the moon to shine in it: for the glory of God did lighten it, and the Lamb is the light thereof. And he shewed me a pure river of water of life, clear as crystal, proceeding out of the throne of God and of the Lamb. In the midst of the street of it, and on either side of the river, was there the tree of life, which bare twelve manner of fruits, and yielded her fruit every month: and the leaves of the tree were for the healing of the nations. And there shall be no more curse: but the throne of God and of the Lamb shall be in it; and his servants shall serve him: And they shall see his face; and his name shall be in their foreheads. And there shall be no night there; and they need no candle, neither light of the sun; for the Lord God giveth them light: and they shall reign for ever and ever."

The city of God is 1,500 miles to the wall or four square (Revelation 21:16). God uses the things ladies like to adorn themselves with; gold, silver, rubies, emeralds, garnet, and other precious stones, for building material for His city. The roads are paved with pure gold. I saw magnificent houses and tall buildings. Earth's structures are limited and imperfect copies of heaven's edifices. There was an area in heaven that was laid out like a plaza with marbled banisters. There were people and angels along street corners singing praises to God like a barber shop quartet. The angels I saw looked like men but they are bigger and light emanates from them. These ones had no wings, and they could walk through walls and buildings just like Jesus; *"And after eight days again his disciples were within, and Thomas with them: then came Jesus, the doors being shut, and stood in the midst, and said, Peace be unto you"* (John 20:26). These angels flew just by God's power and without wings.

I talked with Gabriel. I first met Gabriel the Archangel in my bedroom on one angelic visitation. He awoke me one evening. He's about 8 feet or ceiling height. I estimate him to be about 400lbs and he had no wings. My whole hand was like one finger in the palm of his hand. He came and told me about the future. This happened in 1956; I was 15 years of age. He told me "the Lord is going to honor your country by allowing man to land on the moon". That did not interest me much because I did not feel we had any business up on the moon. He also spoke of my portion in the last day's ministry. That was my first account with Gabriel before seeing him in my heavenly vision. Gabriel is immense and beautiful. He too had no wings, and light came out of his being.

In the city, I met Amy Simple McPherson; she was a famous evangelist who started a ministry called Four Square. Ms. McPherson told me I would be a part of her organization on earth. This came to pass many years later. I shook hands with King David. He was red headed. I also shook hands with Abraham who was a burly big chested man, and he looked like an American State Trooper. He was about 6 feet and 5 inches. I met some people I knew on earth who were now with the Lord. I met my grandfather in heaven; he was already passed on from earth at my age of 2 ½ years. I met

Elijah with whom I spoke, and we were of the same mind. We were both disgruntled about people not honoring God on the earth. The adults in heaven looked about 30–33 years old; seemingly at the age Jesus was crucified. There was a golden chariot parked by a curb with no horse. The angel said to me, "Come on". We got in the chariot and the chariot took off without a horse. It was as though there was an invisible horse. Wherever you wished to go you would get there by simply thinking it, and the chariot would get you there. I looked in the windows of one building, and there was erected a golden stand with an opened Bible on it. This buildings' layout in this beautiful city of God is tiered like a pyramid. God's throne where He sits is positioned at the top of the pyramid and is many miles high.

God is huge. In comparison to Father God's frame, our human structure is almost non-existent. We serve a great big God. I was privileged to approach the throne of God. I looked up and could not see God's face because it was covered with clouds just like clouds cover a mountain top. It was explained to me by the angel that the prayers of mothers for their children were very significant to Father God.

I was made to understand that a part of those clouds were prayers from mothers for their children. The prayers engulfed Father God's head like clouds. In scripture we understand that when God is present, a manifestation of clouds is a natural signature of His immediate company. *"The glory of the LORD abode upon Mount Sinai, and the cloud covered it six days: and the seventh day he called unto Moses out of the midst of the cloud"* (Exodus 24:16).

There are children in heaven; miscarried and aborted ones too. There was a classroom where angels were teaching these children what we were supposed to have taught them. The children were of varied ages and nationality. All these children are safe with the Father. Women who had abortions are forgivable if there is repentance and a turning to God. God makes the penitent heart free. The mercy of God goes to the point of insanity. Hitler, if he turned to God, would have been saved from hell. *"The Lord is not slack concerning his promise, as some men count slackness; but is longsuffering to us-ward, not willing that any should perish, but that all should come to repentance"* (2 Peter 3:9).

Father God is huge. Have you ever seen a fingernail under a stethoscope in your high school biology class? It looks like honeycomb. The ends of God's fingernails look like honeycomb; they looked like diamond and square shapes throughout. I looked at the Father's feet and His toenails were very thick; they looked like honeycomb also. Jesus is from the Father. The Father's throne is in one position and there is a platform. At this point I was with Jesus and He motioned for me to come. From this platform Jesus walked into the side of the Father; He is part of the Father. He walked into His side and He invited me to come but this time I was afraid. I also saw a very scary thing in God's heaven; the four faced creatures. These were the eagle, the man, the calf and the lion. These were extremely fearful to look upon. If I knew I was not in God's heaven it would have scared the life out of me. They spoke to me but I cannot remember what they spoke about. I suppose I was too terrified because they were dreadful to behold. *"And before the throne there was a sea of glass like unto crystal: and in the midst of the throne, and round about the throne, were four beasts full of eyes before and behind. And the first beast was like a lion, and the second beast like a calf, and the third beast had a face as a man, and the fourth beast was like a flying eagle. And the four beasts had each of them six wings about him; and they were full of eyes within: and they rest not day and night, saying, Holy, holy, holy, LORD God Almighty, which was, and is, and is to come"* (Revelation 4:6–8).

You must keep in your mind that these heavenly experiences were in the spirit. I believe I was out of my body but not gone as one would when they die. Unlike a person who is truly gone from earth into heaven, our visions of supernatural experiences enable us to feel earthly emotions that we would not have otherwise felt. I believe that if I was finally gone from earth and was with the Lord, when I was invited into the being of the Almighty God, I would have felt awe as opposed to a fear that terrified.

Concerning visions and revelations the Apostle Paul said, *"It is not expedient for me doubtless to glory. I will come to visions and revelations of the Lord. I knew a man in Christ above fourteen years ago, whether in the body, I cannot tell; or whether out of the body, I cannot tell: God knoweth; such an one caught up to the third heaven. And I knew such a man, whether in the body, or out of the body,*

I cannot tell: God knoweth; how that he was caught up into paradise, and heard unspeakable words, which it is not lawful for a man to utter" (2 Corinthians 12:1–4).

There is a river that comes out of the throne of God, and as it flows away it gets deeper, wider, and bigger. There are trees on both sides of the river, and there are a number of different kinds of fruits on one tree. We do not eat animals; we eat fruit. Jesus said that the leaves of the fruit trees were for the healing of the nations. I did not understand why healing would be needed but I'm sure it is a good thing. John the Revelator said in the book of Revelation, *"And he shewed me a pure river of water of life, clear as crystal, proceeding out of the throne of God and of the Lamb. In the midst of the street of it, and on either side of the river, was there the tree of life, which bare twelve manner of fruits, and yielded her fruit every month: and the leaves of the tree were for the healing of the nations"*(Revelation 22:1-2).

Incidentally, there will be Roman Catholics in heaven, and they are spirit-filled too. I'm not sure as to why I was shown this specifically, but the scripture tells us that all people, tribe, and tongue out of all nations will be in heaven. We often feel that only certain sect of people will be in heaven, but not so. God has His people everywhere. John also said, *"And they sung a new song, saying, Thou art worthy to take the book, and to open the seals thereof: for thou wast slain, and hast redeemed us to God by thy blood out of every kindred, and tongue, and people, and nation"* (Revelation 5:9). Yes dear reader, heaven is a beauty. But, Jesus outshines them all. When I consider the price He paid for our salvation and our eventual redemption from this earth to His glorious heaven, He is most beautiful. The following chapter will give you a glance into the person of Jesus Christ. After all, He is the reason heaven is what it is.

The Person Of Jesus

I had the wonderful opportunity to meet face to face with Jesus. In a vision, I was privileged to look into some interesting attributes and the nature of Jesus as God and man. As a boy I wondered what it would be like to be God. I often times pondered His beginning and what it would be like to actually behold the Almighty. How great is the Creator of the universe? What is He like? Isaiah 40 helps to give a brief description of what Almighty God is like. It serves us well to read these portions of scripture and meditate on them because it is clear, by our actions, that we really do not comprehend the power, authenticity, and sovereignty of the Almighty. We are still here because God is merciful.

Isaiah said, "*Who hath measured the waters in the hollow of His hand, and meted out heaven with the span, and comprehended the dust of the earth in a measure, and weighed the mountains in scales, and the hills in a balance? Who hath directed the Spirit of the LORD, or being His counselor hath taught Him? With whom took He counsel, and who instructed Him, and taught Him in the path of judgment, and taught Him knowledge, and shewed to Him the way of understanding? Behold, the nations are as a drop of a bucket, and are counted as the small dust of the balance: behold, He taketh up the isles as a very little thing. And Lebanon is not sufficient to burn, nor the beasts thereof sufficient for a burnt offering. All nations before Him are as nothing; and they are counted to Him less than nothing, and vanity. To whom then will ye liken God? Or what likeness will ye compare unto Him?* (Isaiah 40:12–18). *Have ye not known? Have ye not heard? Hath it not been told you from the beginning? Have ye not understood from the foundations of the earth? It is He that sitteth upon the circle of the earth, and the inhabitants thereof are as grasshoppers; that stretcheth out the heavens as a curtain, and spreadeth them out as a tent to dwell in: that bringeth the princes to nothing; He maketh the judges of the earth as vanity. (Isaiah 40:21–23). To whom then will ye liken Me, or shall I be equal? saith the Holy One. Lift up your eyes on high, and behold who hath created these things, that bringeth out their host by number: He calleth them all by names by the greatness of His might, for that He is strong in power; not one faileth (Isaiah 40:25–26). Hast thou not known? Hast thou not heard that the everlasting God, the LORD, the Creator of the ends of the earth, fainteth not, neither is weary? There is no searching of his understanding (Isaiah 40:28)."*

Before we were saved through Jesus Christ, we were in darkness. After we got saved we were transformed from the kingdom of darkness to the Kingdom of light. Now we have a choice to walk in the light. We must make up our minds daily to walk in the Light. If we choose to walk in the Light, we will receive the benefit of fellowshipping with each other. When we walk in the light of God's salvation, the precious blood of Jesus Christ, God's Son, is available to wash and cleanse us from all sin. *"The same came for a witness, to bear witness of the Light that all men through him might believe"* (John 1:7). *According to Scripture, we know that*

Jesus Christ is God and He is light and there is no darkness in Him. "In the beginning was the Word, and the Word was with God, and the Word was God. This then is the message which we have heard of him, and declare unto you, that God is light, and in him is no darkness at all" (John 1:1; 1 John 1:5).

I was on the corner of Sanders street and Bay, in my grandmother's old neighborhood, when the thought of what God is like came to me. Well, He showed me. I felt Jesus' Spirit and soul. I did not feel any great power, but He showed me of His great love and great sorrow. When we sin and do our own ways Jesus suffers; He is still suffering even today. There is still much pain in Jesus's heart over lost humanity, because He loves us so very much. Remember, we were all made by Him. We are all His children, but many will be lost at the end of time because they will choose to rebel against their Creator. The Lord is grieved by rebellion and disobedience because He sees the end of such.

Jesus is pure love. Jesus is more innocent than an innocent child, and there is pure love in Him. What is on the horizon for Jesus in the future will be something that will be more difficult for Him to bear than was His crucifixion; that is, the judgment of those who will be sentenced to hell. Jesus is love, and for Him to allow something like this, it will cause Him to hurt more than being crucified, beaten, mocked, or torn. It is man's decisions that will determine his destiny. People have the misconstrued notion that God loves too much to send anyone to hell. Well, this is partially right and partially wrong. God loves indeed; and therefore, He does not send anyone to hell. Man by his own choices here on earth decides where he will spend eternity. This truth is parallel to the law of sewing and reaping. If you plant corn you will most assuredly reap corn. *"Be not deceived; God is not mocked: for whatsoever a man soweth, that shall he also reap"* (Galatians 6:7).

Jesus appears to be the size of a man. The Holy Spirit was His Father in conception of the Virgin Mary, and the Son and the Spirit shared the same blood-type; they are one. Jesus is God; He and the Father are one and this is a mystery. John 1:1–3, 14 says, *"In the beginning was the Word, and the Word was with God, and the Word was God. The same was in the beginning with God. All things were made by Him; and without Him was not anything made that was made. And the Word was made flesh, and dwelt among us, (and we beheld His glory, the glory as of the only begotten of the Father,) full of grace and truth.*" Jesus can do anything and make Himself any size or height with the Father. He can be microscopic or gigantic.

Before coming to earth, the Father and Jesus were overlooking the universe. They were together in what seemed like a plaza – there were activities around them. Father God and Jesus were side by side. They appeared to be the size of two men as we know it on earth. Father God said to Jesus, "It's time now", and Jesus said, "Yes, Father". I wondered what it was time for. Jesus then, in a supernatural form, left His majesty with the Father. After this I saw Jesus lifting off and began drifting away from His Father, from heaven, and from that Plaza. He was now suspended in the air. At this instant, Jesus began to make His journey to earth to save lost humanity. As Jesus left the Father and is proceeding toward the earth, He cried out because He was in pain. He was in pain because He was leaving His Father and was becoming as man. Upon leaving His heavenly domain and embarking upon earth's sphere, Jesus's appearance became smaller and smaller until He entered into the uterus of Mary at about the size of my small finger's nail. He would get nourishment from Mary's body with

God's blood type and be born as we are born human beings. This is what I was shown to have occurred at the event of Jesus's coming to earth in the form of human kind.

Whatever powers Jesus demonstrated in His earthly ministry, He did so as a man who was born of woman and who was completely submitted to the Holy Spirit. His miracles were executed by God the Holy Spirit. He had a great mission to accomplish. He was sent to rescue lost humanity from eternal damnation. John 3:16–17 says, *"For God so loved the world that He gave His only begotten Son, that whosoever believeth in Him should not perish, but have everlasting life. For God sent not his Son into the world to condemn the world; but that the world through Him might be saved."*

During the time of His trial and journey to the cross, Jesus suffered great disgrace. His humiliation was magnified because He was not just another man. Jesus was of heaven's royalty. He was not of this world or kingdom. He was brought to a very low estate in His course of redeeming man. Our portrait of Jesus having a loin cloth on Him during His crucifixion is incorrect. The Romans did not do that. Jesus took on the total humiliation that could be inflicted upon a person; they nailed Him to that tree naked; He drank the full bitter cup. As Jesus was walking through the streets, there were people who did not have any idea of who or what He was. They emptied their chamber pots on Him. The agony of our Lord goes much deeper than what we know. Great evil was done against Him. I saw children throwing rocks at Jesus when He was on that cross. He was despised, rejected, sorrowful, grieved, stricken, smitten, afflicted, wounded, bruised, chastised, oppressed, bound, judged, and cut off.

Isaiah said it truthfully, "*Who hath believed our report, and to whom is the arm of the LORD revealed? For He shall grow up before Him as a tender plant, and as a root out of a dry ground: He hath no form nor comeliness; and when we shall see Him, there is no beauty that we should desire Him. He is despised and rejected of men; a man of sorrows, and acquainted with grief: and we hid as it were our faces from Him; He was despised, and we esteemed Him not. Surely He hath borne our griefs, and carried our sorrows: yet we did esteem Him stricken, smitten of God, and afflicted. But He was wounded for our transgressions, He was bruised for our iniquities: the chastisement of our peace was upon Him; and with His stripes we are healed. All we like sheep have gone astray; we have turned everyone to his own way; and the LORD hath laid on Him the iniquity of us all. He was oppressed, and He was afflicted, yet He opened not His mouth: He is brought as a lamb to the slaughter, and as a sheep before her shearers is dumb, so He openeth not his mouth. He was taken from prison and from judgment: and who shall declare His generation? For He was cut off out of the land of the living: for the transgression of my people was he stricken"* (Isaiah 53:1–8).

They did not nail Jesus through the palm of His hands as some beliefs teach, but they nailed Him through His wrists and feet. He overcame great agony for me, for you, and for the entire world. The description of His tribulation in Isaiah 53 is not there for us to sorrow for Jesus. We need to become sorry for our own souls headed for eternal destruction without Jesus. We must be wise and penitent enough to repent, realize what awesome price Christ paid for our salvation, and accept His provision for our eternal refuge from hell.

At His resurrection, Jesus's body went right through the burial shroud without harming it – it's like laser printing on that cloth. Jesus's magnificence was left with the Father and when He rose from the dead, His majestic position returned to Him. *"Jesus Christ the same yesterday and today and forever"* (Hebrews 13:8). Have you ever thought of who in your life is the most precious, most faithful, most reliable person? Have you ever thought of a person who you could completely absolutely trust at all times, having every confidence that this person loves you unconditionally and would never at any time fail you? Well, for me, this person is Jesus Christ. And how can I be sure that Jesus loves me that much? The answer is clear to me – He gave His life that I would have life. *"Greater love hath no man than this, that a man lay down his life for his friends"* (John 15:13).

In chapter three I told you of my experience in heaven as it was showed me. I showed you a little piece of the beauty of heaven as I saw it. There is also such a place called hell, and you do not want to go there. I feel it is appropriate to set a gulf between chapters three and five with chapter four. In this chapter you acquired insight on some attributes and nature of Jesus as God and man. It is fitting to say that Jesus is that gulf that is fixed between heaven and hell that the one cannot reach to the other. Luke 16:19–26 tells the story well: *"There was a certain rich man, which was clothed in purple and fine linen, and fared sumptuously every day: And there was a certain beggar named Lazarus, which was laid at his gate, full of sores, And desiring to be fed with the crumbs which fell from the rich man's table: moreover the dogs came and licked his sores. And it came to pass, that the beggar died, and was carried by the angels into Abraham's bosom: the rich man also died, and was buried; And in hell he lift up his eyes, being in torments, and seeth Abraham afar off, and Lazarus in his bosom. And he cried and said, Father Abraham, have mercy on me, and send Lazarus, that he may dip the tip of his finger in water, and cool my tongue; for I am tormented in this flame. But Abraham said, Son, remember that thou in thy lifetime receivedst thy good things, and likewise Lazarus evil things: but now he is comforted, and thou art tormented. And beside all this, between us and you there is a great gulf fixed: so that they which would pass from hence to you cannot; neither can they pass to us that would come from thence."* Today, Jesus is waiting to be your Mediator that He might, with His own blood, deliver you from the wrath to come.

Hell Is A Terrible Place

I saw heaven, I saw hell, and I saw the lake of fire. I experienced the bottomless pit. The last thing I was shown while in heaven was the judgment. After the Great White Throne Judgment, Jesus and I embarked upon the shores of a lake that looked like Lake Ontario or Lake Erie. However, it was a lake burning with fire. This place was filled with people and demons, and Satan was there too. Everyone in the Lake of Fire was burning yet their flesh was not consumed. Everyone was filled with hate and bitterness, and everyone was beating on, kicking, and punching on everyone who got in his way. Picture a pyramid in your mind; the mighty on earth is at the top of the pyramid; Hitler, Stalin, Kaddafi, Mussolini; those types of characters, and mighty men who have killed millions for greed and personal gain. In hell great evil men are at the bottom, and they are hated by everyone because everyone blames them for being there, because many followed these mighty men's destructive paths. Everyone in the lake of fire believes it is someone else's fault why they are there.

The first occupants in the Lake of Fire will be the Anti-Christ and the False Prophet. After them, all those who hated and denied Jesus will follow. The Lake of Fire is a literal lake. It is like being on the shores of Lake Ontario and the waters were flames. It is a lake that is pure fire; it is exactly as scripture names it. As this unquenchable fire burned, an unbearable odor emanated from it; it had the stench of sulfur like that from a match when it is freshly lit. The scripture tells us that hell's everlasting fire was *"prepared for the devil and his angels"* and not for mankind (Matthew 25:41). The lake of fire is after the judgment; it is the final place of doom.

When people think of hell they often just think of fire; excessive heat that torments, but it is much more than that. Grave darkness, repulsive odors, hideous creatures, loneliness, a sense of hopelessness and doom are all a part of the judgment of hell. God gave me a good education. He put me in the bottomless pit as part of my education. The Lord brought me down to that abyss with Him.

In one experience, at about the age of 9, I had a spiritual encounter with the Lord where He gave me a tour of hell. My vision occurred when I went to my Aunt Francis' bed to take a nap after school. In the vision I went through her house to the basement and found myself in the underground world. There are different compartments in hell. Hell, right now, has souls in it, and it is in the midst of the earth. I was with the Lord as we toured through this dismal place, but there was also a lady who was receiving the tour along with me. I believe this lady wrote a book on her experience way back in the 60's.

As we went along, we were led down a dirt and gravel path which was an entrance into one of hell's compartments. The lady had more courage than I did. Even though the Lord was with us, I did not want to go into hell. Hell is under our feet; in the belly of the earth. I did not want to take this tour, but the Lord signaled with His hand for me to follow Him, so I forced myself to continue. I was standing back as we entered a tunnel that looked like a coal mine. At this entrance there were two paths that went forth, but I do not recall the difference between the two sections as it pertains to where the other led. I only knew that both paths led down into hell. It is like entering into a deep cave with no exit. The path we took led us to pits that were a certain height in measure on a human being. In these pits you could see nothing; it's like being in a closet with the door shut and the lights off. All the space around us was gross darkness except for the portions we were brought there to see. In this place you could sense that there was someone beside you, but you could see no one. You were not able to touch anyone either, because your hands would go through each other; everyone is in a spirit form.

In hell you constantly hear people screaming, hollowing, crying, and even asking Jesus to forgive them. Jesus told me He can do nothing for man after He dies. *"And as it is appointed unto men once to die, but after this the judgment"* (Hebrews 9:27). Once we leave planet earth, God Almighty is in charge. We cannot say enough prayers to redeem the soul that is headed for hell. Man's final and eternal destiny is determined before he leaves earth. It is chosen by him according to the life he lived. It is as it was with the rich man and Lazarus in Luke 16:19–31. *"There was a certain rich man, which was clothed in purple and fine linen, and fared sumptuously every day: And there was a certain beggar named Lazarus, which was laid at his gate, full of sores, and desiring to be fed with the crumbs which fell from the rich man's table: moreover the dogs came and licked his sores. And it came to pass, that the beggar died, and was carried by the angels into Abraham's bosom: the rich man also died, and was buried; and in hell he lift up his eyes, being in torments, and seeth Abraham afar off and Lazarus in his bosom. And he cried and said, Father Abraham, have mercy on me, and send Lazarus that he may dip the tip of his finger in water, and cool my tongue; for I am tormented in this flame. But Abraham said, Son, remember that thou in thy lifetime receivedst thy good things, and likewise Lazarus evil things: but now he is comforted, and thou art tormented. And beside all this, between us and you there is a great gulf fixed: so that they which would pass from hence to you cannot; neither can they pass to us that would come from thence.*

Then he said, I pray thee therefore, father, that thou wouldest send him to my father's house: for I have five brethren; that he may testify unto them, lest they also come into this place of torment. Abraham saith unto him, they have Moses and the prophets; let them hear them. And he said, Nay, father Abraham: but if one went unto them from the dead, they will repent. And he said unto him, if they hear not Moses and the prophets, neither will they be persuaded, though one rose from the dead."

In the pits were flames that were rising and falling repeatedly. There were demons assigned to these pits in which were human spirits. These demons were there to make sure no one escaped. They were nasty beastly things and they were huge; they looked like a bear, gruesome in appearance and standing on its hind legs and having fury bodies. Their heads and facial structures were hideous. They looked like a pig's head but very ugly – much worse than what might be filmed in a Star Wars movie.

Fear was very much prevalent in hell. The sights of the demons made one gasp in terror. These demons had spears that they used to make sure no one came out of the pit. These demons seem to take extra pleasure in tormenting church leaders. There was a Minister who did not make it to heaven and he was bound in a coffin box, and there were slots in the box. Through these slots or holes, a demon would run the spear into the box, and you would hear the man screaming. These occupants in the pits of hell were spirit bodies and souls. These tormented souls were capable of feeling pain; they could hurt and you could hear them screaming in agony. The demons assigned to these souls took extra pleasure in hurting those who knew about Christ and went the other way. I presume they inflicted greater punishment on them for the positive impact they had on souls lost to the dark kingdom while they were on the earth.

Despite the many visions, revelations, preaching, warnings, and admonitions that are dispersed throughout our world, many people will still end up in hell. This pending doom will not be on account of ignorance or innocence, but it will be as a result of a seared conscience. People choose what and who they want to believe. The sad part about this is that, we do not get to choose heaven after that we have lived an ungodly life on earth. Why did God put a consciousness in us? We have a free will; and with that, He gave us a conscience. We know when we are doing something wrong, but we turn away and do it anyway because nobody sees us. God sees us.

And if it is so that only twelve percent of mankind will escape judgment, how likely are you to be in that number? This world's system as we know it is coming to an end because of its evil: sin, corruption, stupidity, prejudice, immorality, robbery, lies, deception, murders, greed; it's all going to come to an end. *"Now the works of the flesh are manifest, which are these; Adultery, fornication, uncleanness, lasciviousness, Idolatry, witchcraft, hatred, variance, emulations, wrath, strife, seditions, heresies, Envyings, murders, drunkenness, revellings, and such like: of the which I tell you before, as I have also told you in time past, that they which do such things shall not inherit the kingdom of God"* (Galatians 5:19–21). There is only one reason for this degradation of humanity: Satan. Man chooses to take the broad road in life and it only leads to destruction. *"Enter ye in at the strait gate: for wide is the gate, and broad is the way, that leadeth to destruction, and many there be which go in there at: Because strait is the gate, and narrow is the way, which leadeth unto life, and few there be that find it"* (Matthew 7:13-14).

I raised four children, and my wife and I have twelve grandchildren. About eighteen months to two years they start talking, and about three years of age that little child starts lying. If mommy and daddy, grandma and grandpa did not teach them to lie, where did it come from? Is it human nature? No. The brain is like a blank DVD. Whatever you put in it comes out of it. There is something odd that you can't see that's being placed in that little child's mind; the invisible force of evil. The child doesn't know it. He just lies and some parents ignorantly laugh because they think that is cute. No, it is not. It is not cute. It is sorrowful. Something touches your child and you can't even see it. All the resources you have for a weapon against this is the name of Jesus and His word. The demons and Satan have to run from this name Jesus. *"For the weapons of our warfare are not carnal, but mighty through God to the pulling down of strong holds; casting down imaginations, and every high thing that exalteth itself against the knowledge of God, and bringing into captivity every thought to the obedience of Christ"* (2 Corinthians 10:4–5).

In hell everybody blames everybody else for being there; nobody says "it's my fault". Everybody says "somebody else caused me to be here". I saw people being on fire yet their flesh is not being consumed. They are constantly beating on each other with kicking and swearing. That is hell. For those who foolishly scoff at the truth about hell, choosing rather to believe it will be a place for them to party with friends; they are headed for a sad awakening. Satan is the prime target of everyone's anger; they direct their frustrations toward him.

Satan looked half human and half beast. He does not have feet. He looked like a crocodile; no feet but he stands up as it were on his belly and was about 4 feet 6 inches in height and 6 feet 6 inches long with the tail. He had the arms of a man and the head of a man. On his head were holes in the ears area, and it had reptile–like flesh surrounding the holes. Dripping off him was a substance that looked like automobile grease; wherever he touches he made it dirty. He likes to eat, he likes to defecate and he likes to rape. He can be a spirit or a body. He had boils on his face. Satan can give you visions the same as God. When you are in a room and you hear asthmatic breathing; that's Satan. He has asthmatic breathing; that's what he sounds like. If he is in his flesh form you will see grease. This is the image of Satan that was revealed to us as we roamed the corridors of hell.

On another occasion, I had an experience that I call the bottomless pit. I was out in the cosmos. I was in my spirit and I could not see anyone, but I knew there were people out there. I tried clapping my hands to make a sound but my hands went through each other. To the best of my understanding, I would call that the bottomless pit. It was a ceaseless feeling of falling, and I was all alone; Jesus was not physically with me here, though I knew He was monitoring the experience. In this place there was no air to breath. I was in spirit form and there was no hot or cold feeling – it was simply an existence of nothing. It can be very frightening to find yourself all alone in a place you cannot identify, no one to relate with, and you are hopelessly falling into utter darkness. This was my experience. The vision ended and I found myself in my body again and right where I left off before the vision occurred.

Another brief experience I encountered seemed to have occurred for the sole purpose of acquiring the knowledge of how God sees the departed souls of the so called "great men and women" of the earth. These are those who exclude Jesus Christ from their lives. They do great works and acquire much gain, but they do not know God. At one's death there is always an overlay of positive mentions of the deceased. I have never heard of any negative speeches or eulogies put forth concerning a departed soul, especially those who acquired *fame and fortune during their time in the earth. However, "man looketh on the outward appearance, but the Lord looketh on the heart"* (1 Samuel 16:7). In this spiritual encounter, I found myself behind a wall, and there was as it were like a gravel racetrack with grandstands. All the so called "mighty of the earth" were assembled there. They were all walking in procession around the racetrack. They were all there in their pride and glory, but the Lord showed me their souls. They hated everybody, they hated themselves and they hated their comrades who shared in the glory with them. These were the mighty men and women of the earth who harm people and destroy lives.

Scripture tells us what the end shall be for those who deny the Lord and turn away from Him. It tells us of those who do wickedly in the earth. *"For I was envious at the foolish, when I saw the prosperity of the wicked. For there are no bands in their death: but their strength is firm. They are not in trouble as other men; neither are they plagued like other men. Therefore pride compasseth them about as a chain; violence covereth them as a garment. Their eyes stand out with fatness: they have more than heart could wish. They are corrupt, and speak wickedly concerning oppression: they speak loftily. They set their mouth against the heavens, and their tongue walketh through the earth. And they say, 'How doth God know, and is there knowledge in the most High?' Behold, these are the ungodly, who prosper in the world; they increase in riches. When I thought to know this, it was too painful for me; until I went into the sanctuary of God; then understood I their end. Surely thou didst set them in slippery places: thou castedst them down into destruction. How are they brought into desolation, as in a moment! They are utterly consumed with terrors. As a dream when one awaketh; so, O Lord, when thou awakest, thou shalt despise their image. For, lo, they that are far from thee shall perish: thou hast destroyed all them that go a whoring from thee"* (Psalm 73:4–9, 12, 16–20, 27).

Yes, hell is a terrible place and you do not want to go there. The decision is yours. It is not our duty to try to understand God before surrendering our lives to Him. We choose to believe so many other things in this world, why not choose to believe the word of God. Heaven awaits the souls of man and so does hell. It is in our power to make that choice. You have the power to determine your destiny, but you do not get to decide what is on the other side of this life. You cannot receive or enter into the Kingdom of God by logic or by man's understanding. You can enter God's Kingdom only by faith.

God will judge man on an individual level for the decisions he makes and the life he displays. God will also judge whole nations, and unfortunately, America will not be exempted.

Invasion And Judgment On America

I was 15 years old when a terrifying dream came to me. I suddenly awoke from my sleep and I immediately sat up in bed. But, the scene of this disturbing night vision continued projecting before me like a movie on a television screen. I began shaking my head vigorously in an effort to make this frightening episode cease, but to no avail. The vision continued while I sat up in bed, fully awakened.

At the beginning of this vision, I saw prominent government figures over in Moscow making plans on how to overthrow America. This was so very clear to me. It was as though I was looking at all this straight ahead of me. I was having an open vision. Significant government officials were devising ways by which they would destroy America. America is hated. Millions and masses of troops will be launched against us. They will use high tech Korean style combat. While they are talking about destroying us, I saw their minds working. Their plan was that, after they destroy us they will try to kill each other. Each one wanted to be the top dog, and these were China and Russia.

As the vision continued, I saw the invasion of the United States of America by Russia and its former allies with Arab nations on the east coast and China on the west coast. The fact of the Chinese being on the west coast was spoken to me in the vision but I was not made to see them. I was also informed that China's intent was to crush America. This knowledge was relayed to me via supernatural revelation. After this, I saw huge commercial ships. I saw these ships travelling across the Atlantic from the east European ports, the ports of North Africa, and the Middle East. These commerce ships were loaded like cargo ships and they were coming across the Atlantic Ocean. This scene was played out before me as though I was viewing it from a movie screen. Inside these ships of commerce were two by four plywood bunks like on a submarine. They were about two feet apart, and this is where they held their soldiers. The soldiers were sedated. A couple of hundred miles off the coast of America the soldiers became animated again. They ate, used the bathroom, exercised, and got their bodies back in order again. I saw the ships entering the east coast ports of the United States. I was shown New York City. This invasion was carried out in a deceptive manner like that of Pearl Harbor.

As I watched in dismay, the scene changed and the ship came into New York Harbor. A top hatch cover on the ship flew off and the troops barreled out of it like an army of ants. This great army walked defiantly into New York City. The New York City Police Department responded to this unexpected attack with fervent resistance, but to no avail. The comparison of the enemy troop to New York's Police force was like a 40 year old dad clouting his 5 year old son. There was no equality there. New York's police force could not come up against them. The force was wiped out.

The scene changed and I saw the invading troop use the high rise buildings in New York City for prisoner of war camps. They only need a dozen men at street level to keep the prisoners confined. This hostage strategy did not require too many guards. If you are above three stories on these buildings and try to escape you would splat yourself out on the sidewalk. Everything they needed to fight against us we had here; transportation, water, medication, food, they just took everything over. Whatever these enemies needed to accomplish their mandate, New York City already had it all. America even made the bullets that fitted their guns. New York City was an easy target for this intimidating army. They descended upon the city like hail stones, they used everything they wanted, and went wherever they wanted to go.

The scene changed once again and I saw our air force, our cities, our roads, our railways, and our airports all controlled by these enemies. I saw our roads and our cities being bombed and shelled by forces of evil from the other side of the world. This conquering army used American airplanes to bomb America on our territory under their control. I was completely awed and was in disbelief at what I was seeing. How could this be? How could this ever happen to America? America was in grave danger and there was none to help. The greatest nation in the world was becoming like dust in the wind before its enemies.

The invaders are even now plotting to subdue America and establish their empires. However, it is my unwavering hope that this will not happen. God gives visions as a warning to humanity. If we heed His warnings and turn to Him, He will turn back the enemies from us. *"And the LORD said unto Moses, I have seen this people, and, behold, it is a stiff-necked people: now therefore let me alone, that my wrath may wax hot against them, and that I may consume them: and I will make of thee a great nation. And Moses besought the LORD his God, and said, LORD, why doth thy wrath wax hot against thy people, which thou hast brought forth out of the land of Egypt with great power, and with a mighty hand? Wherefore should the Egyptians speak, and say, for mischief did he bring them out, to slay them in the mountains, and to consume them from the face of the earth? Turn from thy fierce wrath, and repent of this evil against thy people. Remember Abraham, Isaac, and Israel, thy servants, to whom thou swarest by thine own self, and saidst unto them, I will multiply your seed as the stars of heaven, and all this land that I have spoken of will I give unto your seed, and they shall inherit it forever. And the LORD repented of the evil which he thought to do unto his people"* (Exodus 32:9-14).

God made a promise to Israel concerning its continued existence as a powerful nation. He said Israel would not be lifted up and driven out of its place ever again. *"Therefore, behold, the days come, saith the LORD, that they shall no more say, The LORD liveth, which brought up the children of Israel out of the land of Egypt; but, The LORD liveth, which brought up and which led the seed of the house of Israel out of the north country, and from all countries whither I had driven them; and they shall dwell in their own land"* (Jeremiah 23:7-8).

The Jews are going to know a lot of pain. Powerful nations are going to force them to do what's not good for them, but God said they are not to do that. They are not to separate their land, but they would give it away just to have some peace. Over 4,000 years of recorded history depicts the Jews' persecution because the word of the one true God came to mankind through those little people. Satan has been trying to kill them ever since. He wants to keep everything secret and hidden but it's not going to work. God is going to stand up and destroy Israel's enemies. This will be a great invasion on the world by God Himself. Evil mankind is in pursuit of destroying Israel, and when they touch Israel, God is going to retaliate with great destruction. The head of the State of Iran wants to wipe Israel off the face of the earth, and he speaks just like Hitler, but it's not going to happen.

I also believe that the United States of America will be upheld by the living God. I believe the whole world combined will not defeat this union, and it is not because we have thousands of atomic bombs, but it is because of the gospel of Christ preached by this nation to many nations. America has done more for charity and Christianity than the rest of the world combined.

This vision occurred in 1956 and at that time I saw Buffalo and New York; United States armies utilizing M1 Garand rifle, M1 Carbine, Thompson submachine gun, and Colt 45 Sidearm. I saw that everybody had, what I called at that time, a machine gun; it's the M16 today. The helmets were reminiscent partially in appearance to the German helmets of World War I and II. The shape of the helmets our army wore was similar to the German helmet. I saw "Buffalo, New York" and I saw the street sign "Niagara and Busty". Troops were involved in door to door combat like Europe in World War II. I saw our forces defeated on the field.

Our defeat is on account of our spiritual adultery. In the word of God, the Lord had an important conversation with Solomon: *"And the LORD appeared to Solomon by night, and said unto him, I have heard thy prayer, and have chosen this place to myself for a house of sacrifice. If I shut up heaven that there be no rain, or if I command the locusts to devour the land, or if I send pestilence among my people; If my people, which are called by my name, shall humble themselves, and pray, and seek my face, and turn from their wicked ways; then will I hear from heaven, and will forgive their sin, and will heal their land. Now mine eyes shall be open, and mine ears attent unto the prayer that is made in this place"* (2 Chronicles 7:12-15).

Christianity and the Jewish faith are getting closer and closer together. We used to mock the Jews years ago, and that was evil on our part. Nothing has changed God's mind about Israel and the Jews. His promise is still the same. There are Christian leaders who are teaching people that the Christian church is now the new Israel. No. God is going to deal with Israel again and He is going to lift them up. I was in Israel in the year 2003. The wealth of the world is going to be poured into Israel in the last days, and Russia and the Arab world are going to try to destroy Israel for great bootie. There is nothing there of great bootie right now. They have the high technology industry and the armaments industry. There's no greater wealth than Israel's, and God will make that evident. But, in the very near future there is going to be a lake of oil under Israel. It is going to frustrate the Arab world. They are going to be aggravated, because they have already claimed that is their land and that is going to be their oil.

Now you know the reason why Russia and its former communist allies and the Arabs are going to attack Israel. In the book of Ezekiel 37 and 38, the cup of the Lord's anger will be filled concerning the nations of the earth, and He is going to defend Israel. It will be like Rode Island being attacked by the rest of the United States of America where Rode Island utterly destroys America. One sixth of their armies will walk back home; the rest will be dead by Israel. There will be nuclear weapons used; Israel is going to use them. The Israelis will not be lifted up again, driven out or taken into slavery. God will fight for the Israelis. The Bible says that Jerusalem is God's and it belongs to the Jews; nobody else, and nobody is going to take it away from them without being damaged by God.

In this vision I was brought to a beach scene in the Mediterranean in Israel. Authorities apparently did a job of roping off a particular area with tapes like that which policemen use to mark off a crime scene. They had the shore marked off with danger signs, and there were ships that were washed up on the shore. These ships were radioactive hot. Israel is going to defend itself with God's hand behind them. I saw this period of time that we are living in, and at the same time I saw the invasion of America.

I saw the period of time with the terrorist and the bombings. The next victims of the terrorists will be our schools. They will kill our children, they will demoralize the adults, they will demoralize the nation of America; they will work to take America down in that way. But God is going to do some defensive work. There is going to be some damage to America of course. Over three thousand people died in the twin towers but it is my faith that America will not be defeated. This will come by our turning back to God.

Our first President, George Washington, had a similar experience like that of my vision which was more of a nightmare. If you ever heard of George Washington's vision of America; it depicts some of the same which I saw. George Washington is a man who honored God. In 1777 he was losing a host of men in the battle; they were starving to death, they contracted pneumonia and things of that nature. British bullets and shells were not killing his soldiers then but it was disease, starvation, and death by freezing. Because he was a man who honored God, he got in his little farm house there in Valley Forge and sought the Lord God. It is now a national park and is part of our heritage.

An account of President Washington's vision concerning America's invasion can be found online. He bares testimony in his journal of what he saw and of what happened. He was at his desk and he sensed the presence of the Lord. He looked up and an angelic being was suspended off the floor. At the time there were 13 colonies in rebellion. The last portion of George Washington's vision of America is World War III and America is being invaded on our soil and our people are being killed. Do a search online and read and understand how the Lord gives visions to His people as warnings and for the benefit of those who will obey Him.

"And it shall come to pass in the last days, saith God, I will pour out of my Spirit upon all flesh: and your sons and your daughters shall prophesy, and your young men shall see visions, and your old men shall dream dreams: and on my servants and on my handmaidens I will pour out in those days of my Spirit; and they shall prophesy: and I will shew wonders in heaven above, and signs in the earth beneath; blood, and fire, and vapour of smoke: the sun shall be turned into darkness, and the moon into blood, before the great and notable day of the Lord come: and it shall come to pass, that whosoever shall call on the name of the Lord shall be saved" (Acts 2:17-21).

If you watch television or read the newspaper, you'll see that Satan is on his last rampage to destroy the Church. There are scandals of the Roman Catholic Church and its Priests indulging in immoral activities with minors. There are scandals concerning the non-Catholic faith Ministers and their indulgence with prostitutes. It was foretold back in 1987 that there would be an attack on the leadership of churches. There has been recent news that they have found the tomb of Jesus; suggesting that His remains have been found; therefore, He did not rise. Satan is a liar. There was also the Davinci code that suggests that Jesus was married to Mary Magdalene, and that in this marriage offspring was produced. What insanity. We know that Jesus Christ was never married to anyone. The scripture tells us that Jesus was cut off; He has no generation because He came to do a job in behalf of His Father. He did not come to live on earth and raise a family. Jesus came to save lost humanity. When He accomplished His task, He ascended back to His father. *"He was taken from prison and from judgment: and who shall declare His generation? For He was cut off out of the land of the living: for the transgression of my people was he stricken"* (Isaiah 53:8).

In the aftermath of the great invasion on America, I saw the citizens of America humble themselves and got on their knees before the Lord God. They picked up the weapons the armies left or threw away and began to fight against the invaders with divine help from above. With angelic assistance, the invaders were defeated and driven out. This scene ended my horrific vision.

The Lord gave me several visions; some short and some lengthy. In each vision a message is communicated to me as His messenger. Over the years of receiving visions from the Lord, I am sure I have forgotten some of what I saw. I am now a senior, so though my reporting is perhaps delayed in man's eyes, I believe the time is now for its full disclosure. I am making every effort to reveal what the Lord will allow me to reveal.

Approximately 25 years ago, I saw, in a vision, an earthquake in Los Angeles. The city was leveled with the exception of the Angeles Temple. The temple belongs to God, but a portion of it was damaged because there were imperfections somewhere. I recon the whole structure would have been held together if all was well. God is the Judge of that. The building was damaged but not as severe as the rest of the city; the city was leveled.

I also saw in a vision a military convoy pull into the Vatican Plaza, and anyone dressed in a clergy's uniform; Priests or Nuns, were all machine gunned and killed. I assume this will occur after the rapture.

Anyone with a clergy's uniform would be killed (Catholic or non-Catholic). Enemy armies pulled in to kill them. The Pope went into exile in France and they killed him there. Heads of states; Italy, Germany and France will be assassinated. Communism will try to take over Western Europe.

I do not believe the rapture is far off. The book of Revelation chapter 8 tells us of two heavenly bodies that will strike the earth; one is a comet and it is called wormwood. The Russian word Chernobyl translates in English as wormwood. I believe it was around 1995 that scientists had a scenario of what they would do if a comet or asteroid struck the earth. If earth is hit by a rock and the rock had a nuclear tip on it and it falls to the earth, the debris would spread wide across the earth and that would be poison for humanity. The worst thing man has ever done is to make nuclear radiation; there is no cure for it; you die. The Bible speaks of millions dying from poisoned water. If we have 20 tons of debris falling in our bodies of water or reservoirs, what will we drink? *"And the name of the star is called wormwood: and the third part of the waters became wormwood; and many men died of the waters, because they were made bitter"* (Revelation 8:11).

The second heavenly body; an asteroid, would take out 1/3 of the earth. In 2003 I got home from work and my wife had supper ready for me. I took my supper and went out to the television room and turned the news on. The commentator said Nassau has just discovered an asteroid on a collision course with earth and it should reach earth Feb. 3rd, 2017. Of course my ears popped up. I'm flipping through all the channels but the government zipped it right off. There's another prediction of 2036; another asteroid on a collision course, but I believe the Lord will be here at the time and He'll take care of that one. A third of the earth and everything; all animals, humans, and trees will be destroyed.

According to scientists, they discovered what happened to all the dinosaurs, the mammoths and all those huge animals; an asteroid hit in Yucatan peninsula; the equal to about 50,000 nuclear weapons, and this blasted the effects all across the earth. *"And when he had opened the seventh seal, there was silence in heaven about the space of half an hour. And I saw the seven angels which stood before God; and to* them were given seven trumpets. And another angel came and stood at the altar, having a golden censer; and there was given unto him much incense, that he should offer it with the prayers of all saints upon the golden altar which was before the throne. And the smoke of the incense, which came with the prayers of the saints, ascended up before God out of the angel's hand. And the angel took the censer, and filled it with fire of the altar, and cast it into the earth: and there were voices, and thunderings, and lightnings, and an earthquake. And the seven angels which had the seven trumpets prepared themselves to sound. The first angel sounded, and there followed hail and fire mingled with blood, and they were cast upon the earth: and the third part of trees was burnt up, and all green grass was burnt up. And the second angel sounded, and as it were a great mountain burning with fire was cast into the sea: and the third part of the sea became blood; and the third part of the creatures which were in the sea, and had life, died; and the third part of the ships were destroyed. And the third angel sounded, and there fell a great star from heaven, burning as it were a lamp, and it fell upon the third part of the rivers, and upon the fountains *of waters; and the name of the star is called Wormwood: and the third part of the waters became wormwood; and many men died of the waters, because they were made bitter. And the fourth angel sounded, and the third part of the sun was smitten, and the third part of the moon, and the third part of the stars; so as the third part of them was darkened, and the day shone not for a third part of it, and the night likewise. And I beheld, and heard an angel flying through the midst of heaven, saying with a loud voice, Woe, woe, woe, to the inhabiters of the earth by reason of the other voices of the trumpet of the three angels, which are yet to sound!"* (Revelation 8).

When the millennium is here, as in the book of Isaiah where it speaks of the time of the Lord's rule, there will still be people born at that time in this world. There will be those who are saved after the rapture and after the tribulation period. There will be procreation; there will still be children being born. It's hard for me to comprehend this because of the hell we've been through as the human race. This will be a time of great beauty; no diseases, no bad weather. If you work 24 hours a day, you would not have aches and pains. There will be no boredom during the millennium. The millennium earth is not heaven, but the way things are right now in earth it will be heaven to the inhabitants. There will be continual building. Those who lived their lives in Christ will be the ones most blessed in this time.

"And there shall come forth a rod out of the stem of Jesse, and a Branch shall grow out of his roots: and the spirit of the LORD shall rest upon him, the spirit of wisdom and understanding, the spirit of counsel and might, the spirit of knowledge and of the fear of the LORD; and shall make him of quick understanding in the fear of the LORD: and he shall not judge after the sight of his eyes, neither reprove after the hearing of his ears: but with righteousness shall he judge the poor, and reprove with equity for the meek of the earth: and he shall smite the earth: with the rod of his mouth, and with the breath of his lips shall he slay the wicked. And righteousness shall be the girdle of his loins, and faithfulness the girdle of his reins. The wolf also shall dwell with the lamb, and the leopard shall lie down with the kid; and the calf and the young lion and the fatling together; and a little child shall lead them. And the cow and the bear shall feed; their young ones shall lie

down together: and the lion shall eat straw like the ox.

And the sucking child shall play on the hole of the asp, and the weaned child shall put his hand on the cockatrice' den. They shall not hurt nor destroy in all my holy mountain: for the earth shall be full of the knowledge of the LORD, as the waters cover the sea. And in that day there shall be a root of Jesse, which shall stand for an ensign of the people; to it shall the Gentiles seek: and his rest shall be glorious" (Isaiah 11:1-10).

Whatever you desired to be in this present life; whatever your aspirations; whatever fulfills your heart and mind, you will be able to accomplish it during the time of the millennium. Those who just made it over the line will not have this privilege. A lot of people say "well just before I die I'll ask the Lord to save me". Well you will be losing out. You will lose out on a great deal.

A young man gave a testimony of somebody who wanted to convert him to the Muslim faith. For those of you who have friends or family who are followers of Mohamed, you can ask them one question; "Do they have any Benny Hinns over there?" Have you ever seen anything on television of the Muslim cleric praying and anybody being healed of anything? You've never heard of it, have you? Only the true and living God is able to perform true and lasting miracles.

Let me point out this one thing; there is proof of the existence of supernatural evil. Those of you who have children, their minds at baby and early childhood are like a blank computer. What comes out of it is whatever was put into it. Suddenly that little child starts lying. Some parents pass that off as being cute, but that evil slime Satan has got that child. It's time for America to awake and stand for righteousness according to God's dictates.

The same nations that hate Israel hate America also. We have the same enemies. One of the reasons the Arab Muslims hate us so is because of America's immorality. In our commercials, women posing practically naked to sell an automobile is something these people hate, and they look upon us as satanic people. America has left her first love; Jesus Christ and His ways, and she has turned to gross immorality. But scripture tells us that God is a jealous God. *"Ye shall not go after other gods, of the gods of the people which are round about you; (For the LORD thy God is a jealous God among you) lest the anger of the LORD thy God be kindled against thee, and destroy thee from off the face of the earth"* (Deuteronomy 6:14-15). God wants what belongs to Him. He will do whatever it takes to reclaim His own, and this is simply because He is so abundant in mercy. The Lord chastens who He loves and corrects who He delights in. *"For whom the Lord loveth he chasteneth, and scourgeth every son whom he receiveth"* (Hebrews 12:6). He loves and delights in America. He also tells us that the nation who forgets Him will be turned into hell; not by Him, but by that nation's own doings. *"The wicked shall be turned into hell, and all the nations that forget God"* (Psalm 9:17).

In 1998, the Lord gave a friend of mine a profound vision and I want to share it with you. I am not at liberty to disclose my friend's identity but I can share the experience. The following is the word for word report of my friend's night vision from the Lord:

Early morning of January 7, 1998, the Holy Spirit came to me in a dream. He brought me to the entrance of the property where I resided at that time. As I stood on my parking lot of this property, near to the public walkway, I noticed, in the not too distant view, an individual coming toward me. As the individual got closer I saw it was a young man. With mine eyes fixed on him like a stethoscope, my focus was drawn to an object he carried in his hand. I soon recognized that he was carrying a loaf of bread. Immediately after identifying the bread, the Holy Spirit spoke saying, "Famine is coming to America". After this, my focus was redirected and I beheld the young man's garment as he got closer. I discovered that he was dressed in clothing that was torn, old, pale-colored, and rugged. At this instant the Holy Spirit spoke again saying, "This famine will first be reflected in the way people dress". Once again my focus was redirected, only this time I was now seeing myself; almost as if I stood outside of myself viewing myself. I found that I was dressed in a beautiful formal garment; an outstanding brilliant red attire. I was somewhat astonished at its beauty, because I wondered why I was so formally dressed standing casually at the gate of my residence. Immediately the Holy Spirit spoke again saying, "This famine will not touch those who are in Christ Jesus". At these words my eyes were opened and I realized I was in my bed feeling as if I was never asleep. At this moment, while wide awake, the Holy Spirit spoke once more, and His words filled the room leaving me no doubt. The Lord spoke saying, "Perilous times are coming".

The points that stood out in my friend's record of the vision are the words the Holy Spirit spoke. These are: famine is coming to America, this famine will be first reflected in the way people dress, this famine will not touch those who are in Christ Jesus, and perilous times are coming. If famine is eminent for America, what do you suppose might be the fate of other nations? Wherever you are friend, your safety from the distresses that are now coming upon the earth is only found in Jesus Christ. Jesus Christ is your New Testament Ark of Safety. Get on board and stay on board.

Matthew 24 outlines very clearly for us what the end-times hold for humanity: *"And Jesus went out, and departed from the temple: and his disciples came to him for to shew him the buildings of the temple. And Jesus said unto them, See ye not all these things? Verily I say unto you, there shall not be left here one stone upon another that shall not be thrown down. And as he sat upon the Mount of Olives, the* disciples came unto him privately saying, tell us, when shall these things be? And what shall be the sign of thy coming, and of the end of the world? And Jesus answered and said unto them, Take heed that no man deceive you. For many shall come in my name, saying, I am Christ; and shall deceive many. And ye shall hear of wars and rumours of wars: see that ye be not troubled: for all these things must come to pass, but the end is not yet. For nation shall rise against nation, and kingdom against kingdom: and there shall be famines, and pestilences, and earthquakes, in divers places. All these are the beginning of sorrows.

Then shall they deliver you up to be afflicted, and shall kill you: and ye shall be hated of all nations for my name's sake. And then shall many be offended, and shall betray one another, and shall hate one another. And many false prophets shall rise, and shall deceive many. And because iniquity shall abound, the love of many shall wax cold. But he that shall endure unto the end, the same shall be saved. And this gospel of the kingdom shall be preached in all the world for a witness unto all nations; and then shall the end come. When ye therefore shall see the abomination of desolation, spoken of by Daniel *the prophet, stand in the holy place, (whoso readeth, let him understand).*

Then let them which be in Judaea flee into the mountains: Let him which is on the housetop not come down to take anything out of his house: Neither let him which is in the field return back to take his clothes. And woe unto them that are with child, and to them that give suck in those days! But pray ye that your flight be not in the winter, neither on the sabbath day: For then shall be great tribulation, such as was not since the beginning of the world to this time, no, nor ever shall be. And except those days should be shortened, there should no flesh be saved: but for the elect's sake those days shall be shortened. Then if any man shall say unto you, Lo, here is Christ, or there; believe it not. For there shall arise false Christs and false prophets, and shall shew great signs and wonders insomuch that, if it were possible, they shall deceive the very elect. Behold, I have told you before.

Wherefore if they shall say unto you, Behold, he is in the desert; go not forth: behold, he is in the secret chambers; believe it not. For as the lightning cometh out of the east, and shineth even unto the west; so shall also the coming of the Son of man be. For wheresoever the carcase is, there will the eagles be gathered together. Immediately after the tribulation of those days shall the sun be darkened, and the moon shall not give her light, and the stars shall fall from heaven, and the powers of the heavens shall be shaken: And then shall appear the sign of the Son of man in heaven: and then shall all the tribes of the earth mourn, and they shall see the Son of man coming in the clouds of heaven with power and great glory. And he shall send his angels with a great sound of a trumpet, and they shall gather together his elect from the four winds, from one end of heaven to the other.

Now learn a parable of the fig tree; When his branch is yet tender, and putteth forth leaves, ye know that summer is nigh: So likewise ye, when ye shall see all these things, know that it is near, even at the doors. Verily I say unto you, this generation shall not pass, till all these things be fulfilled. Heaven and earth shall pass away, but my words shall not pass away. But of that day and hour knoweth no man, no, not the angels of heaven, but my Father only. But as the days of Noe were, so shall also the coming of the Son of man be. For as in the days that were before the flood they were eating and drinking, marrying and giving in marriage, until the day that Noe entered into the ark, and knew not until the flood came, and took them all away; so shall also the coming of the Son of man be. Then shall two be in the field; the one shall be taken, and the other left. Two women shall be grinding at the mill; the one shall be taken, and the other left.

Watch therefore: for ye know not what hour your Lord doth come. But know this, that if the goodman of the house had known in what watch the thief would come, he would have watched, and would not have suffered his house to be broken up. Therefore be ye also ready: for in such an hour as ye think not the Son of man cometh. Who then is a faithful and wise servant, whom his lord hath made ruler over his household, to give them meat in due season? Blessed is that servant, whom his lord when he cometh shall find so doing. Verily I say unto you, that he shall make him ruler over all his goods. But and if that evil servant shall say in his heart, My lord delayeth his coming; and shall begin to smite his fellowservants, and to eat and drink with the drunken; the lord of that servant shall come in a day when he looketh not for him, and in an hour that he is not aware of,

And shall cut him asunder, and appoint him his portion with the hypocrites: there shall be weeping and gnashing of teeth".

Our enemies' invasion of our territory is God's judgment on America for turning away from Him and for not heeding His prophets. We have become grossly rebellious against the Almighty, and we are far removed from the faith of our forefathers. In scripture, every time Israel fell away from God He dealt with them by causing their neighbors to come in and overthrow them. *"Blow ye the trumpet in Zion, and sound an alarm in my holy mountain: let all the inhabitants of the land tremble: for the day of the LORD cometh, for it is nigh at hand; a day of darkness and of gloominess, a day of clouds and of thick darkness, as the morning spread upon the mountains: a great people and a strong; there hath not been ever the like, neither shall be any more after it, even to the years of many generations. A fire devoureth before them; and behind them a flame burneth: the land is as the Garden of Eden before them, and behind them a desolate wilderness; yea, and nothing shall escape them. The appearance of them is as the appearance of horses; and as horsemen, so shall they run. Like the noise of chariots on the tops of mountains shall they leap, like the noise of a flame of fire that devoureth the stubble, as a strong people set in battle array.*

Before their face the people shall be much pained: all faces shall gather blackness. They shall run like mighty men; they shall climb the wall like men of war; and they shall march everyone on his ways, and they shall not break their ranks: neither shall one thrust another; they shall walk everyone in his path: and when they fall upon the sword, they shall not be wounded. They shall run to and fro in the city; they shall run upon the wall, they shall climb up upon the houses; they shall enter in at the windows like a thief. The earth shall quake before them; the heavens shall tremble: the sun and the moon shall be dark, and the stars shall withdraw their shining: and the LORD shall utter his voice before his army: for his camp is very great: for he is strong that executeth his word: for the day of the LORD is great and very terrible; and who can abide it?

Therefore also now, saith the LORD, turn ye even to me with all your heart, and with fasting, and with weeping, and with mourning: and rend your heart, and not your garments, and turn unto the LORD your God: for he is gracious and merciful, slow to anger, and of great kindness, and repenteth him of the evil. Who knoweth if he will return and repent, and leave a blessing behind him; even a meat offering and a drink offering unto the LORD your God? Blow the trumpet in Zion, sanctify a fast, call a solemn assembly: gather the people, sanctify the congregation, assemble the elders, gather the children, and those that suck the breasts: let the bridegroom go forth of his chamber, and the bride out of her closet. Let the priests, the ministers of the LORD, weep between the porch and the altar, and let them say, Spare thy people, O LORD, and give not thine heritage to reproach, that the heathen should rule over them: wherefore should they say among the people, Where is their God?" (Joel 2:1–17).

America has gotten itself three nasty scars: 1–we have killed countless millions of babies by abortions performed on our grounds, 2–we have dealt wrongly with the American Native Indians as though they were nothing. It took an act of Congress to call the Native Indians human beings, and, 3–the cruel slavery of African Americans. God deals with individuals and their sins one on one, but when a nation sins He judges the whole nation. So, if you are wondering why America is appointed unto judgment from the Almighty by means of invasion by Russia and their communist allies; these are some reasons.

Those of you who worry about money, a new house, a new luxury vehicle, forget it. If you have food in your refrigerator, your family is healthy, and you love one another you are wealthy. This money god that so many crave will soon become toilet paper. The Lord God is going to see to it unless we as a nation repent and do the works that demonstrates we have changed for the better.

It is time dear reader for us to repent and return to the Almighty God. He wants to revive us. *"If my people, which are called by my name, shall humble themselves, and pray, and seek my face, and turn from their wicked ways; then will I hear from heaven, and will forgive their sin, and will heal their land"* (2 Chronicles 7:14).

The Coming Great Revival

Restitution, renewal, restoration, stimu-
lation, revitalization, reinforcement,
recovery; all these describe the true meaning of
revival. When we are revived we are changed
from the lesser to the better, from the least to
the best. Contrary to some beliefs in the church,
a two or three day weekend of spiritual confer-
encing and charismatic highs do not a revival
make. I believe a true revival is the pure work of
the Holy Spirit's presence in, upon, and among
men. It is the Spirit's presence to the degree that
repentance from sin and self is evoked and sur-
render to Christ is evident.

As a little boy, the first time my parents
took me to church was at St. Francis on Bay
Street in Rochester. I also went to grammar

school there. I was 2 ½ to 3 years old and it was around Easter time on a nice sunny day. The inside of the sanctuary was huge; around 35 feet off the floor, and so I'm looking around expecting the man in charge to be big. The Priest emerged with two altar boys from a side room door, and I was disappointed. I thought maybe he was God, but he wasn't God. I expected someone huge and powerful but he was just a man. God is great. He is awesome and so are His works. When He revives our lands we will know it. It will be a work that no man can lay claim to. It will be a work that only the Almighty could do.

Israel thought their plight was hopeless but God spoke to His servant Ezekiel in a vision and declared to Ezekiel what He will do for His people Israel. *"The hand of the LORD was upon me, and carried me out in the spirit of the LORD, and set me down in the midst of the valley which was full of bones, and caused me to pass by them round about: and, behold, there were very many in the open valley; and, lo, they were very dry. And he said unto me, Son of man, can these bones live? And I answered, O Lord GOD, thou knowest. Again he said unto me, Prophesy upon these bones, and say unto them,*

*O ye dry bones, hear the word of the LORD.
Thus saith the Lord GOD unto these bones;
Behold, I will cause breath to enter into you,
and ye shall live: and I will lay sinews upon you,
and will bring up flesh upon you, and cover you
with skin, and put breath in you, and ye shall
live; and ye shall know that I am the LORD.
So I prophesied as I was commanded: and as
I prophesied, there was a noise, and behold a
shaking, and the bones came together, bone to
his bone. And when I beheld, lo, the sinews
and the flesh came up upon them, and the skin
covered them above: but there was no breath
in them. Then said he unto me, Prophesy unto
the wind, prophesy, son of man, and say to the
wind, Thus saith the Lord GOD; Come from
the four winds, O breath, and breathe upon
these slain, that they may live. So I prophesied
as he commanded me, and the breath came into
them, and they lived, and stood up upon their
feet, an exceeding great army. Then he said
unto me, Son of man, these bones are the whole
house of Israel: behold, they say, our bones are
dried, and our hope is lost: we are cut off for
our parts. Therefore prophesy and say unto
them, Thus saith the Lord GOD; Behold, O
my people, I will open your graves, and cause*

you to come up out of your graves, and bring
you into the land of Israel. And ye shall know
that I am the LORD, when I have opened your
graves, O my people, and brought you up out of
your graves, and shall put my spirit in you, and
ye shall live, and I shall place you in your own
land: then shall ye know that I the LORD have
spoken it, and performed it, saith the LORD"
(Ezekiel 37:1–14).

Kim Clement, a Prophet of God, and The
Elijah's List attest to the following: The Isuzu
Street Revival of 1904 is going to happen all
over again starting with the African Americans.
The latter rain blessing that will come upon
America will begin with the African American
Christian church. They will lead the way of the
last outpouring of the Holy Spirit and the rest
of God's people will pick up thereafter. I know
this because the Lord has revealed this to me in
a vision also. Man with his segregation, bias,
and prejudice is irrelevant to what God will
do. Our indifferences toward each other are all
nonsense. Many people do not like to hear this,
but King Solomon was a black man. The man
who carried the cross of Jesus was a black man,
and so was the first convert to Christianity, the
Ambassador to Ethiopia; he was a eunuch in

Israel. The Carthaginian Generals, Hannibal and Archibald were Africans and converts to Christ. African Americans have a mighty heritage in the gospel of Christ. Besides, God will use whoever He wills to do His work. With God there is no respect of persons. *"There is no respect of persons with God"* (Romans 2:11). All we need to do is to fall in line with His plan.

In my life, God has hired me a couple times for intercessory prayers and healing of His people. I was about 9 years old and my Aunt Francis was a sainted woman; beautiful lady. She was a single lady and she lived in my grandmother's house. I was outside with my cousin one summer afternoon. Into the evening, I heard the adults saying that Aunt Francis almost had a stroke. They were crying, and my aunt could not walk or get out of bed. Her arm would not work anymore so I was upset. Doctors usually come to a person's house at those times, and such was the case with my Aunt Francis. The doctor walked up the driveway, so I ran up to the doctor and looked up at him and said, "Doctor, my Aunt Francis had a stroke. Can you fix her?" I loved my Aunt Francis. By the look of the doctor's eyes and his facial expression, I knew he could do nothing. I and my cousin Lowie, who is 18 months older than I, decided that we had better pray for Aunt Francis because the doctor cannot do anything. So we got on our knees there in the driveway and began doing the ritualistic "our Father prayer". While we were doing that, I heard words I had never heard the sounds of before, and I know the general sounds of several languages. I stopped and looked at my cousin and he was laughing at me. He said, "What are you talking about?" I said, "What are you talking about?" But the strange words were coming from my mouth. Yes, it was me; I was speaking in tongues. I did not know what I was saying.

My other aunt came to the second story side of the house and she signaled at me in the driveway. I went in to see my Aunt Francis, and I told her that the Lord told me to do this; that is, to give her a little wine and tell her to go to sleep. She did just that and she was healed. Apparently, a little wine is good for the body and it is found in scripture. I am not promoting wine however, but I responded in faith to a word of knowledge from the Holy Spirit, and my Aunt Francis was healed. God uses willing ready vessels. That could very well be you.

I was working in security at US Air and a co-worker of mine contracted bronchitis a lot. She would be pale looking, hacking, coughing, and all fevered up. At break time I went over to her and told her I would like to pray for her. She agreed willingly. I placed my hand on her shoulder and asked for the Lord to heal her. Ten minutes went by and I was back to work. I looked over at my co-worker and she was smiling and laughing and was pink colored again. I asked her if something had happened. She said "yes, I feel good". The goodness of the Lord leads man to repentance. Repentance is a part of true revival. *"Despisest thou the riches of His goodness and forbearance and longsuffering; not knowing that the goodness of God leadeth thee to repentance?"* (Romans 2:4).

In a vision I saw a baseball stadium, and there were crowds there just like at a Billy Graham Crusade or a Red Wings game; there were chairs out in the infield. I was at the age of 15 here also. The Lord showed me that there will come a time of a great outpouring of the Holy Spirit. In this ball park, there were two main isles that led to the main platform. What I saw was a 24 hour church service. One church would moderate for two hours and then another for two hours and another, and so on. There was a continual flow of churches rotating with praying and singing. They were singing, praying, and praising God. What I saw was amazing. These meetings were so powerful that families took their dead in their caskets from the funeral homes over to the ball park. At the time it was the Red Wings stadium here in Rochester, but it might very well be the Frontier Field that is here now.

The families took their dead in their caskets and lined them up down the aisles from the pitcher's mound to about center field. No preacher went down to these; people just continued offering up praises unto God and the dead was raised. The embalmed bodies rose up with new life. People were being healed and demons were being cast out. I am from the Roman Catholic background, and I did not see any Catholic Priests or Nuns on the platform, but I saw them in the audience praising God. I saw this happen right here in Rochester in this vision.

The Lord also revealed to me that before the rapture there will be a great outpouring of the Holy Spirit on the Roman Catholic Church, the Greek Orthodox, the Russian Orthodox, the Lebanese Maronite Christians and the Ethiopian Coptic Church, and this will provoke the main line protestant Church to jealousy. It is my presumption that this jealousy will lead us to our knees in seeking God as never before. It is His will that we all be conformed to the image of His dear Son, Jesus Christ.

Conclusion

When the Lord God gives man visions, He has a purpose in mind. God desires to draw man to Himself and bless him abundantly. It had been His plan from the beginning of time. When Adam and Eve sinned, God gave us Jesus Christ that He might reconcile man back to Himself. Visions are given as part of God's plan to conform man to the image of His Son, Jesus Christ. He speaks to us so we would know His will for our lives, and visions are part of the ways He does this.

Time is a short moment in comparison to eternity. Every man must pass through the vale of time. At the end of that passage he will enter into eternity. What that eternity looks like for each man will directly depend on how he lived in time.

It is God's utmost desire that every man would enter into His heaven; into His eternal rest. Heaven is a beautiful place and the Lord Jesus Himself is gone to prepare this place for us. He wants us to be with Him forever. We are so soaked through with our humanity that it is sometimes mystical to some to see man in such a place called heaven. It is perfect. It is peaceful. It is eternal, and I plan to be there. How about you?

Jesus is all that heaven is and then some. He is the best description of what perfection is in all its beauty. Jesus is hated by many because they do not understand Him. Man has forgotten that God is the Potter and we are the clay. The clay does not tell the Potter what to do. Jesus loves us more than we will ever be able to love or be worthy of. On one occasion in scripture, Saul of Tarsus, in his relentless pursuit to overthrow early Christians, breathed out cruelty in the name of God, and the Lord appeared to him. The Lord said, *"Why persecutes though Me? It is hard for thee to kick against the pricks"* (Acts 9:5; 22:7). We lose out when we decide we do not want Jesus Christ. It is to our benefit to get to know the Lord who made us. He is our Father, He is awesome, He loves unconditionally, and He will come again for those who love Him. He has bridged the gap between hell and heaven, now all we need to do is to choose.

Hell was made for Satan and his angels. Imagine having a child you love so deeply. You see your child heading down the wrong path; a path that is sure to destroy him. You do all in your best effort to rescue that child, but the child is not willing to be delivered, because he thinks his way is right, but you know better. *"There is a way that seemeth right unto a man, but the end thereof are the ways of death"* (Proverbs 16:25). This is what the Lord experiences with humanity. We are His children. Hell awaits all who rebels against Father God.

The story of the prodigal son in Scripture paints the perfect picture of the Father's heart toward His creation. This son rebelled at first, but fortunately for him, he came to himself and repented. And what did he find at the end of his repentance? He found a father who was ready and willing to forgive, deliver, and restore him. *"And he said, a certain man had two sons: and the younger of them said to his father, Father, give me the portion of goods that falleth to me.*

And he divided unto them his living. And not many days after the younger son gathered all together, and took his journey into a far country, and there wasted his substance with riotous living. And when he had spent all, there arose a mighty famine in that land; and he began to be in want. And he went and joined himself to a citizen of that country; and he sent him into his fields to feed swine. And he would fain have filled his belly with the husks that the swine did eat: and no man gave unto him. And when he came to himself, he said, How many hired servants of my father's have bread enough and to spare, and I perish with hunger! I will arise and go to my father, and will say unto him, Father, I have sinned against heaven, and before thee, and am no more worthy to be called thy son: make me as one of thy hired servants. And he arose, and came to his father. But when he was yet a great way off, his father saw him, and had compassion, and ran, and fell on his neck, and kissed him. And the son said unto him, Father, I have sinned against heaven, and in thy sight, and am no more worthy to be called thy son. But the father said to his servants, Bring forth the best robe, and put it on him; and put a ring on his hand, and shoes on his feet: and bring hither the fatted calf, and kill it; and let us eat, and be merry: for this my son was dead, and is alive again; he was lost, and is found. And they began to be merry" (Luke 15:11–24). The Lord waits to do the same for every man who will turn unto Him before it is eternally too late. Hell is real dear friend, and you don't want to go there.

God sends judgment upon mankind for only one reason; that man would repent of his evil. *"With my soul have I desired thee in the night; yea, with my spirit within me will I seek thee early: for when thy judgments are in the earth, the inhabitants of the world will learn righteousness"* (Isaiah 26:9). God wants to revive the earth; as many as are willing. Revival begins in the heart. It is a work that God desires to do in individuals, and by His Holy Spirit, He wants to ignite and unite His chosen people. Revival comes only to the willing contrite heart. Is that you? If you have not made Jesus your Lord, do so today. Eternity is fast approaching, and the Spirit and the Bride is now saying to Jesus, come (Revelation 22:17).

Resources

The resources listed below are not an endorsement by the author of this book but are there for you to broaden your scope on prophetic disclosures and that you execute your own research and draw your own conclusions.

Book, Final Quest by Rick Joyner

Book, Heaven is for Real by Todd Burpo

Book, Heaven is so Real by Choo Thomas

Book, The Late Great Planet Earth by Hal Lindsay

Book, Bound to Lose, Destined to Win by Earthquake Kelley

George Washington's vision at www.civil-liberties.com/pages/prophesy

Prophetic disclosures at www.elijahlist.com

Prophetic disclosures at www.kimclement.com

About The Author

LOUIS NICOLOSI was born in Rochester, NY, USA where he lived for the greater part of his life. Louis was converted to Christ at the early age of 9. He had a loving family and raised one of his own. He is a retiree from General Motors where he rendered his services for many years.

Louis loves the Lord Jesus and he is burdened at the evil that has so filled the earth. Through his own experiences, he understands that God communicates with man through various visions. Louis considers himself a servant and messenger of the Lord for these end-times. It is with this understanding that he faithfully delivers the messages of the Lord unto you.

In a world that today seems intolerable to the unadulterated word of God, Louis passionately embraces the whole scripture as it was sent from God to man. He feels God still speaks and writes through His true servants today. He feels man determines his eternal destiny, and Warnings From Heaven has risen for such a time as this. It serves to aid in directing man to his eternal home.

It is Louis' prayer that you will read Warnings From Heaven with an open heart before the Lord. He desires that, by it, your life will be positively affected to the praise of the glory of God's Kingdom through Jesus Christ our Lord.